GENIUS REVISITED:

HIGH IQ CHILDREN GROWN UP

Creativity Research

Mark A. Runco, Series Editor

Achieving Extraordinary Ends: An Essay on Creativity, by Sharon Bailin
Counseling Gifted and Talented Children, edited by Roberta M. Milgram
Creative Thinking: Problem-Solving Skills and the Arts Orientation,
 by John F. Wakefield
Divergent Thinking, by Mark A. Runco
Genius Revisited: High IQ Children Grown Up, by Rena Subotnik, Lee Kassan,
 Ellen Summers, and Alan Wasser
More Ways Than One: Fostering Creativity, by Arthur J. Cropley
Perspectives on Creativity: The Biographical Method, by John E. Gedo and
 Mary M. Gedo

In preparation:
Beyond Terman: Longitudinal Studies in Contemporary Gifted Education,
 edited by Rena Subotnik and Karen Arnold
Contexts of Creativity, by Leonora Cohen, Amit Goswami, Shawn Boles, and
 Richard Chaney
Creativity: Theories, Themes and Issues, by Mark A. Runco
Creativity and Affect, edited by Melvin Shaw and Klaus Hoppe
Creativity in Government, by Thomas Heinzen
Nurturing and Developing Creativity: Emergence of a Discipline, Volume 2,
 edited by Scott G. Isaksen, Mary C. Murdock, Roger L. Firestien, and
 Donald J. Treffinger
Problem Finding, Problem Solving, and Creativity, edited by Mark A. Runco
*Understanding and Recognizing Creativity: Emergence of a Discipline, Volume
 1,* edited by Scott G. Isaksen, Mary C. Murdock, Roger L. Firestien, and
 Donald J. Treffinger

GENIUS REVISITED:

HIGH IQ CHILDREN GROWN UP

Rena Subotnik, Lee Kassan, Ellen Summers, and Alan Wasser

ABLEX PUBLISHING CORPORATION
NORWOOD, NEW JERSEY

Printed in the United States of America

Library of Congress Cataloging-in-Publication Data

Genius revisted : high IQ children grown up / by Rena Subotnik... [et
al.].
   p. cm. — (creativity research)
  Includes bibliographical references and indexes.
  ISBN 0-89391-978-0 (hard.) — ISBN 1-56750-005-6 (pbk.)
  1. Gifted children—Psychology—Longitudinal studies. 2. Gifted—
Psychology—Longitudinal studies. 3. Gifted children—Education—
Longitudinal studies. 4. Gifted—Education—Longitudinal studies. 5.
Hunter College, Elementary School—Students. 6. Hunter College. High
School—Students. I. Rubotnik, Rena Faye. II. Series.
BF723.G5G365 1993
153.9'8—dc20   93-9168
                                                     CIP

Ablex Publishing Corporation
355 Chestnut St.
Norwood, NJ 07648

CONTENTS

Acknowledgments

Retrospective studies that span over 40 years are steeped in personal and social history and are immensely interesting to conduct. At the same time, they are enormously labor intensive. Without the assistance of the people and institutions that are mentioned below, this research could not have been carried out as comprehensively.

The first component of the study involved the adaptation of the Terman mid-life questionnaire for use with a contemporary middle-age population of grown-up high-IQ children from Hunter College Elementary School (HCES). This work was conducted with the invaluable assistance of Brondi Borer, David Karp, and Elizabeth Morgan. Much of the time-consuming search for graduates from the 1940s and 1950s was ameliorated by the efforts of Anthony Camarda, who searched through New York City Telephone books, and by *Our Town* (a Manhattan neighborhood newspaper), and *The New York Times*, with descriptive blurbs encouraging HCES graduates to contact us. The collected questionnaire data were quantified and matched with the Terman data stored in the Inter-University Consortium for Political and Social Research (ICPSR). Making the data comparable was a challenging task, masterfully accomplished by Paula Diamond, Elizabeth Morgan, and David Karp, with the assistance of Nancy Larkin at the Hunter College Academic Computing Center. The final analyses of the questionnaire data were reported by Rena Subotnik, David Karp, and Elizabeth Morgan in the March 1989 issue of *Roeper Review*.

The four authors of *Genius Revisited* initiated the interview component of the project and were deeply involved in every aspect of this book. We began by interviewing over 100 HCES graduates. Both Lisa Hurwitz and Louise Fox provided able assistance as supplemental interviewers. Debra Kaplan transcribed the interview tapes and, along with Ella Lariviera, helped us with the preliminary identification of quotations that were eventually selected for inclusion in the manuscript.

At Hunter Elementary School, we were given the support and encouragement of former principals Jane Navarre Piirto, Arthur Pober, and Elliott Koreman, and the current principal Evelyn Castro, who has kindly written a Foreword to this manuscript. Former Director of the Hunter College Campus Schools (which include HCES and Hunter College High School) Evelyn Jones Rich and current Director Anthony Miserandino provided advice and suggestions, and Dr. Miserandino has also added his thoughts to a Foreword to this volume. We would like to thank the Hunter College High School librarian, Harriet Aufses, and the Elementary School librarian, Regina Brauer, for their assistance in providing historical documents that were essential to establishing the context of the study.

The first author is extremely grateful for the temporal and financial support she received from the administration of Hunter College. Dean Hugh Scott provided her with release time at the Hunter College Campus Schools to conduct various evaluation, curriculum and research projects, and provided some philosophical thoughts in a Foreword to this book. The opportunity for regular interaction at the school facilitated conducting this project as she became a familiar and recognized presence in the building. Former President Donna Shalala provided a generous amount of seed money for the project, which was further augmented by a Shuster Faculty Grant.

The third author extends her appreciation to Dr. Zachary Summers for his patience and valued suggestions, to the staff of the Great Neck, New York library's main branch for their kind assistance, and to colleagues in the English Department of C.W. Post for their support.

We would like to thank Mark Runco, Series Editor, for his excellent advice, our parents for being wise enough to send us to Hunter College Elementary School, and our partners or spouses for being emotional anchors and inspirations. Finally, the authors express their gratitude to the participating graduates of Hunter College Elementary School, who provided us with some of the most interesting hours of our professional lives, and without whose time and insights this book could not have been written.

The Authors

Dr. Rena F. Subotnik, specialist in gifted education at Hunter College and research/curriculum consultant to the Hunter College Campus Schools, has been awarded research and training grants with the National Science Foundation, the Javits Grant program of the U.S. Department of Education, and the Spencer Foundation. She was the winner of the 1990 Early Scholar Award of the National Association for Gifted Children and currently serves on the editorial board of the *American Educational Research Journal* and as chairperson of the Research and Evaluation Division of the National Association for Gifted Children. She is a 1959 graduate of Hunter College Elementary School.

Lee D. Kassan, M.A., is a psychotherapist in private practice in New York City, specializing in the treatment of gifted adults and adolescents. He is a Fellow of the American Institute for Psychotherapy and Psychoanalysis and was formerly Director of the Adolescent Program at Odyssey House, a therapeutic community treating drug abuse. He is a 1956 graduate of Hunter College Elementary School.

Ellen S. Summers, M.S., a prize-winning poet and author of short stories, reviews, and articles featured in various literary journals and periodicals including *The New York Times*, *Gargoyle*, and *Confrontation*, teaches undergraduate composition, creative writing, and literature at the C.W. Post campus of Long Island University. A graduate of Hunter College and Brooklyn College, she taught in the New York City and Nassau County school systems and at Queensborough Community College. She was a student teacher at the Hunter College Elementary School.

Alan B. Wasser, Chairman of The Executive Committee of the National Space Society, was a broadcast journalist for 13 years, (writer for ABC News, Senior Editor for CBS, Director of News and Public Affairs for Capital Cities radio station WPAT). He owned and operated a successful international business firm for 11 years and is now an independent computer consultant. He entered Hunter College Elementary School in 1943, at age 3, and graduated in 1951. He then graduated from the Bronx High School of Science and attended the Massachusetts Institute of Technology and New York University (graduated in 1962 and elected to Phi Beta Kappa). He is the author of articles in publications such as *Space World*, *Ad Astra*, and *Space News*.

Foreword

It is a genuine pleasure and honor to have a chance to write a few words introducing *Genius Revisited*. This is a longitudinal study that adds significantly to our understanding of what happens when high-ability children who receive a special education grow up.

For almost half a century, our portrait of gifted students (particularly gifted students grown up) has been based upon the longitudinal study of about 1,500 high-IQ children begun by Lewis Terman in 1921 and continuing to this day. The portrait that emerged from these studies was considered to be the template for what gifted children were like and how they developed as adults. It was difficult to determine, however, whether the Terman study outcomes were generalizable, or whether, instead, they reflected a Northern California culture, or a particular era in American history.

This book by Rena Subotnik, Lee Kassan, Ellen Summers, and Alan Wasser does much to add to that portrait by reporting a longitudinal study using a different sample of high-ability children of a more recent era, all of whom attended Hunter College Elementary School (HCES) in New York City. This remarkable school designed for high-ability students, with a talented and committed faculty, created as ideal an environment for intellectual stimulation that was possible at the time. The number of parents that were clamoring to get their children into HCES made it possible for the school to select, very carefully, not only children with the highest IQ scores, but also children who fit what they believed to be appropriate personality and motivational dimensions.

Does the portrait of high-ability students identified by Terman change with this new information? Certainly it changes with regard to women. As a product of a very different era, virtually all female graduates of Hunter College Elementary School between 1948–1960 had careers, many with Master's or Doctorate degrees. Only half of the Terman women were career oriented.

One of the great joys of this book is that you can hear the Hunter graduates talking about themselves, their families, their school, and their opinions, in their own words. These long and well-chosen passages bring to life the otherwise staid statistics of employment, motivation, underachievement, and so on.

The authors were disappointed to discover that although this sample succeeded admirably in traditional terms, with its share of physicians, lawyers, and professors, there were no creative rebels to shake society out of its complacency or revolutionize a field. Yet, there are very few such individuals alive in any particular era. The statistical odds against any one of them having graduated from one elementary school in New York City is great. Whether the "creative rebel" would have survived the selection process at Hunter, or any similar school, is one of those remaining questions that should puzzle and intrigue us.

The authors raise another interesting and challenging question: whether what is bad for the individual may be good for the society. In other words, a set of conditions which create chronic unhappiness may be necessary to create the obsessive concern with a particular goal and the single-minded drive and motivation to achieve that goal. Norbert Weiner, in his book *The Autobiography of an Ex-Genius*, detailed his unhappy family life with a domineering father and enough personal problems to be in and out of mental institutions. Yet, it was this Norbert Weiner who gave the world cybernetics that revolutionized our society. What if he had had a happy family life with a warm and agreeable father? One is left to wonder whether Weiner would have had the drive and motivation to make this unique contribution.

The same question can be posed for these Hunter College Elementary School graduates. Are many of them too satisfied, too willing to accept the superior rewards that their ability and opportunity have provided for them? What more could they have accomplished if they had a "psychological worm" eating inside them—whether that worm was low self-concept or a need to prove something to someone or to the world—that would have driven these people to greater efforts. What if their aptitudes had been challenged in a more hard-driving manner, like Weiner's experience, into the development of a specific talent? This book raises many significant, sometimes disturbing issues. It is a fine contribution, and I believe it will become a standard reference in the field.

James J. Gallagher
Kenan Professor of Education
University of North Carolina at Chapel Hill

Being identified as an intellectually gifted child is a blessing that may also be a burden. By virtue of their outstanding potentialities, intellectually gifted children have a capacity for high performance, differing from their peers in abilities, talents, interests, and often psychological maturity. However, as a by-product of being labeled intellectually gifted, there are high expectations for impressive accomplishments in adulthood. The academic demands placed on intellectually gifted students by their own initiative and by the expectations set for them by parents, educators, and friends are considerable. As perhaps the most versatile and complex of all human groups within our society, the potentialities of the intellectually gifted child must be appropriately nurtured; intellectual talent cannot survive educational neglect and apathy.

The Hunter College Elementary School (HCES) provides planned educational programs and services specifically for intellectually gifted students in response to their idiosyncratic cognitive and psychological needs. The classification and placement of students into special programs does not remove the responsibility for adapting instruction to individual differences, even within this seemingly homogeneous exceptional population. Instructional strategies currently employed at HCES accommodate the educational needs and learning styles of all of its students. This commitment requires the provision of progressive and relevantly differentiated curriculum, in addition to individualized instruction.

Subotnik, Kassan, Summers, and Wasser examined graduates of the Hunter College Elementary School to determine whether or not their adult attainments were commensurate with their identified childhood potential, and whether or not their educational experiences at HCES had an influence on what they did or did not accomplish as adults. No valid guarantee could ever be issued that intellectual giftedness alone provides assurances of meaningful achievement as an adult. Nevertheless, the volume's probe of how graduates of HCES fared with regard to their attainments as adults offers insightful clues as to which factors, both in and out of school, appear to have positive or negative influences on what is pursued and accomplished by high-IQ children grown up.

Hugh J. Scott
Dean
Division of Education
Hunter College
City University of New York

Being selected to attend a specialized school carries many burdens: parental expectations, varied teacher demands, and labeling by peers. At the same time, schooling experiences can set the pace for future self-expectations, hopes, and dreams. Attending the Hunter College Elementary School is concurrently a great gift and a great burden.

The authors of this study set out to describe the impact of this schooling experience as reflected upon by a special cohort of students now grown up. The data offered in this study both complement and extend the knowledge bases of two types of research literature: research on gifted children, and research on adult development over the life span. Both areas are important to our work in educating and nurturing talented children.

One of the significant contributions of the present volume is material on and insights into the impact of giftedness and adult development on the lives of women. A key chapter of the text deals with gender differences, role models, and the impact of the Hunter mythos of academic rigor and achievement at all cost, and above all other pursuits (i.e., family and noncareer activities). The varying degrees of conflict between family expectations and academic demands are made clear in the voices of the graduates as they reflect back on their school experience from the perspective of midlife. I hope the emotional toll of life choices detailed in this chapter on women is in (sharp) contrast to the emotional future of great possibility offered to women (and men) today at the Elementary School. I believe we have learned something in recent years about the inclusive, expansive, and nonsexist nature of caring, compassion, and intellectual rigor at the Hunter College Campus Schools.

The authors raise some disturbing issues regarding the purposes of schools for the gifted. Indeed, just what is the contemporary rationale for funding schools or programs for the highly gifted student? If one is looking to such an institution as a source of leading students towards societal leadership (or, as the authors suggest, "a path to eminence"), then the Hunter College Elementary School of the past failed to realize such an aspiration. Indeed, this goal may well be beyond the reach of any elementary school.

Yet, schooling for the intellectually gifted is a critical need for society. Identifying and nurturing talent is important for both the individual and the society which will benefit from the creativity and talent of such individuals (as the authors illustrate, perhaps at the cost of personal pain to some individuals). Critical to this schooling process is deciding when and how much effort should be directed at an early age toward nurturing specialized talents. As the authors indicate, this is not an easy decision to make.

Given the dynamics of individual motivation, the limited resources of any schooling experience, and the historical moment of the Hunter experience, the Campus Schools' rationale of the past is very much present today: educating for the broad intellectual and skill development of its elementary students. Building upon this foundation, the High School seeks to enhance students' commitment to intellectual rigor and growth, develop opportunities for specialization, and commitment to caring and compassion. Will such a rationale foster more students down the path towards genius? The research literature and the current study would indicate that such a condition is a necessary but not sufficient condition to move students into making groundbreaking discoveries or toward professional eminence. Does it follow then that such schools should not exist? Or at least, not at public expense? I would vigorously argue against both reactions.

The world of Lewis Terman's children has changed, the world of the Hunter Elementary cohort is changing, and the world of tomorrow will be different for today's children. Genius at any age carries the promise and possibility of an era. Schools like Hunter have an obligation to prepare their students for a life of intellectual integrity and openness to shaping the future agenda of society.

Our students will be entering a multicultural world with diminishing resources and global issues which have an impact on their daily lives. Society needs "Hunter-like" students. Schooling of less quality is a failure of administrative vision for the leadership needs of tomorrow's children.

Anthony Miserandino, Ph.D.
Director, Hunter College Campus Schools

This volume describes the history, dilemmas, and revelations that unfolded during Hunter College Elementary School's (HCES) nascent years, beginning in 1941. Our current school population carries on the tradition of challenging faculty and administration to create and implement programs based upon both current research-based practice and each child's unique talents.

There are a great many similarities between the HCES of today and the HCES of the 1940s and 1950s. The children are equally brilliant, and the curriculum continues to emphasize enrichment, exploration, and discovery. The present faculty and administration, however, have introduced contemporary societal concerns into the school's philosophy, curriculum, scheduling, and instructional methodology. More emphasis is being placed on skills of communication, such as sharing success, resolving issues, clarifying arguments, and identifying common goals and visions. It is important to us that our school be a stronghold of compassion and understanding.

These humanistic values can only be borne from an educational environment that respects cultural diversity and exists in complete collaboration with parents and the home environment. Hunter College Elementary School seeks to enhance our role as a laboratory school by celebrating both cultural and ethnic differences and excellence in the pursuit of knowledge.

Our modern perspectives are reflected in the children's exposure to the use of technology in the exploration of interdisciplinary themes. Our library and computer laboratory serve as resources to the study of the environment, patterns in mathematics and science, political issues, or aesthetics. Our curriculum is more carefully articulated across and through the grades than was true in the earlier days of Hunter College Elementary School, but the strong emphasis on the visual arts remains an integral part of our tradition.

At HCES in the 1990s we are busy reading and conducting research, welcoming visitors from around the nation and the world, mentoring the next generation of New York City teachers, and writing and editing a widely distributed annual newsletter, *Hunter Outreach*. Our students, faculty, staff and administration are creating a new era in the history of Hunter College Elementary School.

Dr. Evelyn W. Castro
Principal
Hunter College Elementary School

chapter 1
Introduction and Overview

Gifted programs have been established in schools in order to address the academic and social needs of children whose accomplishments or demonstrated potentials surpass what is available in the regular curricular program. The specter of elitism is raised, however, when programs designed for gifted children mirror what is available in the private sector for children admitted on the basis of high socioeconomic status rather than special aptitude. Research-based, long-term studies of effective identification and programming policies for children who exhibit exceptional academic and general problem-solving skills are, therefore, essential as a base for identification policies and curricula in gifted education.

A recent interest in longitudinal research, as demonstrated in the policy statements of the National Research Center for the Gifted and Talented (Gubbins & Reid, 1991), is a positive sign that the educational community is prepared to learn from experiences with the special programs and alternative methods of identification that the field of gifted education has been accumulating since the 1920s. A forthcoming collection of studies will report on the long-term outcomes of identification and programming models including the Torrance Tests of Creativity, the Renzulli Triad Model, the Purdue Three-Stage Model, SAT-M, grade point average, and science contests, among others (Subotnik & Arnold, 1993). This research perspective, when joined with retrospective studies of eminent individuals, should provide the field with a more comprehensive picture of the development of talent and the fulfillment of gifted potential.

This volume summarizes a study which was designed to assess the outcomes of early identification and schooling for a group of highly gifted children. The subjects of the investigation are graduates of one of America's most selective educational institutions, the Hunter College Elementary School. HCES developed as an outgrowth of a series of experiments and philosophical statements reflecting the political and social history of the United States in the first half of the 20th century, and was created in 1941 to serve children with IQ scores at least two standard deviations above the mean.

Despite considerable controversy, IQ test scores remain the most heavily weighted source of information for admission of children to gifted programs in the United States. We propose that the reported reflections of individuals in their 40s and 50s, who were selected at approximately age 4 for special instruction on the basis of high IQ scores, can provide insight into the development of future educational options for gifted students. Our objective is to contribute these unique perspectives to the literature which describes and analyzes the long-term outcomes of educational decisions concerning the identification and education of gifted children. In this first chapter we present a brief discussion of IQ tests and a description of the background variables on the high-IQ individuals who serve as subjects of this study.

IQ TESTS

An IQ score indicates quantitatively how well a person negotiates a set of tasks comprised in an intelligence test, compared to other individuals of the same age. IQ tests come in two forms: one designed for group administration, the other to be conducted on a one-to-one basis. Although the individual form is expensive and labor-intensive, it is considered more rigorous than the group form, reflecting more accurately a child's aptitude. Although the group tests were designed originally to help sort students, soldiers, or workers into academic and occupational tracks, the individual intelligence test was used to identify individuals who deviated extraordinarily from the mean in terms of general intelligence (Chapman, 1988) (see Additional Readings).

One of the most widely used individual IQ tests has been the Stanford-Binet, first administered on a nonpilot basis in 1916. Up through its most recent revision (S-B IV, 1986), the Stanford-Binet has included items which test vocabulary, comprehension, analogies, similarities and differences, verbal and pictorial completion, recognition of absurdities, and recall of numbers from short-term memory. The test is scored in a standardized form, with 100 serving as the median or 50th percentile. Each revision has become more rigorous; scoring in the 99th percentile on the 1916 version was slightly less difficult than on the 1937 (L-M) version. When originally conceived, the test was designed to identify childhood genius, predicting not only outstanding academic achievements, but professional success as well.

THE HUNTER COLLEGE ELEMENTARY SCHOOL STUDY

The Hunter College Elementary School study was designed to address the question of adult productivity within a population comprised of high-IQ subjects socioeconomically similar but geographically and generationally different from the cohort established in the 1920s by Lewis Terman, father of the Stanford-Binet test, to verify his predictions of academic and professional success. The HCES graduate group described in this book was considered by Terman as a good comparison group for his cohort of "geniuses" (Seagoe, 1975). The mean IQ of the Hunter sample was 157, or approximately 3.5 standard deviations above the mean, with a range of 122 to 196 on the L-M form. (Although a score of 122 IQ does not fit the admissions cut-off of two standard deviations above the mean, there was a very small number of exceptions made by Hunter's admissions officers. No documentation exists to provide reasons for these exceptions.)

Each class at Hunter College Elementary School from the years 1948 to 1960 contained about 50 students, yielding a total possible population of 600 graduates for our study. Because the only addresses available were those obtained when the study participants were pupils at the school, acquiring access to individuals and records was difficult. Fortunately, many of these addresses proved to be still valid. By consulting area telephone books, many additional Hunter graduates were located. Others were found through advertisements in local newspapers (e.g., *The New York Times*), high school alumni newsletters, and word of mouth. Despite the significant period of time that had passed, 35% of the total population of 1948-1960 HCES students ($N = 210$) completed and returned study questionnaires.

SUMMARY OF QUESTIONNAIRE OUTCOMES

Each participant in the study completed a 17-page questionnaire largely based on the 1951/1955 survey conducted by Lewis Terman and his associates. Some demographic data are presented below, followed by highlights of the survey which reflect the issues addressed in this book. For further information about questionnaire responses, see Subotnik, Karp and Morgan (1988) and Subotnik and Borland (1992).

Marital Status

Approximately 90% of the former Hunter students were married; 15% of those individuals have been divorced at least once. Ten percent of the group never married.

Religious Affiliation

The Hunter group is approximately 62% Jewish, although they describe themselves as Jews more in terms of ethnic identity than religious practice. The group, as a whole, is not religious.

Educational Attainments

Over 80% of the study participants held at least a Master's degree. Furthermore, 40% of the women and 68% of the men held either a Ph.D, LL.B., J.D., or M.D. degree.

Occupation and Income

Only two of the HCES women identified themselves primarily as homemakers. Fifty-three percent were professionals, working as a teacher at the college or pre-college level, writer (journalist, author, editor), or psychologist. The same proportion of HCES men were professionals, serving as lawyers, medical doctors, or college teachers. The median income for men in 1988 was $75,000 (range = $500,000) and for women $40,000 (range = $169,000). Income levels were significantly different for men and women, even when matched by profession. For example, the median income for male college teachers or psychologists was $50,000 and for females, $30,000.

Political Affiliation

For the most part, the Hunter graduates who participated in this study described themselves as liberal rather than conservative. Over 70% tended to vote as Democrats.

Physical and Mental Health

A majority of the respondents described their health at midlife as "very good," and less than 10% reported having "considerable difficulty" with mental health problems at some point in their lives. There was no correlation between the incidence of mental health problems and IQ within the group.

Factors Influencing Accomplishment of Life Goals

Over 85% of the respondents identified adequate education and superior mental ability as contributing significantly to the accomplishment of their life goals. Secondarily, mental stability, good personality, and persistence were reported as playing a pivotal role.

Family Socioeconomic Status

The graduates of Hunter College Elementary School in the 1940s and 1950s tended to come from homes where the father was a professional (68%) and the mothers were either professionals (48%) or homemakers (31%). Furthermore, when asked to describe the socioeconomic status of their homes, 57% identified their childhood family's financial situation as adequate, 19% as abundant. Eighteen percent remembered their economic situation as being limited and 5% very limited. Reflecting the overwhelmingly middle-class milieu in which they lived, 75% of the parents did not interfere with their children's choice of vocation as long as the choice was from among the traditional professions. Schoolwork was addressed in the same way—with little interference, and high but unstated expectations.

Valuing Success

One section of the questionnaire was designed to elicit respondents' ratings of their desire to succeed in a number of areas, such as leadership, finance, sociability, and academics. As can be seen in Table 1.1, the domains deemed important for most of the participants were leadership and academic pursuits, more so than material acquisition or a rich social life.

These data were further supported by the participants' responses when rating the aspects of their life from which they derived the greatest satisfaction. The most common responses are given in Table 1.2 (more than one aspect could be listed).

Table 1.1

Area	Slightly or not at all interested	Very or extremely interested
Leadership	21%	53%
Finance	18%	42%
Sociability	25%	34%
Academic Pursuits	12%	62%

Clearly, there was no consensus of opinion in this group as to what accounts for individual accomplishment.

Honors, Awards, and Creative Productivity

Much like the Terman subjects, the Hunter graduates received special honors for their activities at work and in the community. In fact, 24% reported having received a minimum of at least three honors thus far, and an additional 39% mentioned having received at least one honor.

The questionnaire included an open-ended item concerning creative work produced by the participants. Although 35% did not list any creative activities, the remaining 65% did, with 28% in the arts, 15% in writing, and the remainder in science, architecture, engineering, and education.

When asked whether they were becoming more like their mothers or their fathers, only 31.9% of the sample, both men and women, reported that they were becoming more like their mothers. Yet from

Table 1.2

Aspects of Life from which Participants Derived Greatest Satisfaction	Percentage of Responses
children	47%
work	39%
marriage	37%
recognition for accomplishments	29%
social contacts	11%
religion	4%
income	3%
community service	3%

among those who had produced the greatest amount of publicly acknowledged creative work as adults (e.g., published writings or grants awarded for scientific projects), 75% of the males and 45% of the females reported that they were becoming more like their mothers (Subotnik & Borland, 1992).

Life Success

The respondents also listed factors they associated with life success. The three highest ranking factors did not elicit many responses but included:

- peace of mind   16%
- happy home   14%
- interesting work   12%

Three factors associated with high achievement motivation were ranked even lower:

- living up to one's ability   9%
- recognition for accomplishments   4%
- striving for a goal   2%

Planning for Accomplishment of Goals and Purposes

The final variable investigated with the questionnaire explored the participants' views on the importance of establishing a life plan in order to accomplish definite goals. The Hunter graduates apportioned themselves in the following manner:

- 2% had no definite life plan, and tended to drift from goal to goal;
- 16% tended to be satisfied with just "getting by," addressing a goal or problem as it came along;
- 40% considered themselves in the middle of this scale;
- 41% said they had a well-established plan for their life; and
- 1% saw their life completely integrated toward a definite goal.

In sum, the study participants are productive professional people, and well-integrated into their communities. As a group they are liberal and nonreligious in their outlook. From their perspective, they are neither particularly materialistic, nor social climbers. They report enjoying their work and their families and do not arrange their lives in such a way as to make a predetermined goal the focus of their existence.

The Hunter graduates are quite similar to the Terman cohort at midlife (Subotnik, Karp, & Morgan, 1989). Both enjoyed good mental and physical health, stable interpersonal relationships, and impressive professional credentials. The comparison study conducted by Subotnik et al. (1989) concluded:

> The most dramatic differences evidenced between the Terman and Hunter groups are those found between the groups of women. The increased availability of occupational and educational opportunities has led to a shift in life satisfaction and success values closer to those exhibited by the Terman and Hunter men (Sears & Barbee, 1977). In fact, in more recent interviews, even the Terman housewives expressed some regret for having neglected their professional development (Eccles, 1985).

> In general, both studies support the notion that high intelligence as measured by IQ is a useful variable in predicting productivity in academics and the professions but not the aesthetic or political arenas (Goertzel & Goertzel, 1962; Terman & Oden, 1959). Yet, nonintellective factors such as motivation, flexibility, social intelligence, ethnic culture, and chance, play an essential role in differentiating whether or not an individual will live up to his or her intellectual potential (Clausen, 1981; Goleman, 1980; Oden, 1968; Seagoe, 1975; Walberg, Rasher & Hase, 1983). Like the Terman group, none of the members of the Hunter group has (yet) achieved the status of a revolutionary thinker. Individually initiated radical change may need to emerge out of obsession, and few of the Hunter graduates describe an obsessive relationship with work or avocational interests. (Subotnik et al., 1989, p. 143)

THE INTERVIEWS

In addition to the questionnaire, 74 study participants were individually interviewed by the authors. This one- to-two-hour in-person or telephone discussion allowed participants to elaborate on topics such as life goals, creative achievement, satisfaction with accomplishments, and the role a high IQ might have played in the way they had lived their lives. Fifteen more Hunter graduates chose to respond to the interview questions in writing. The excerpts in this book come from these taped and written interviews.

The Interview questions addressed the following areas:

- positive and negative memories of the school;
- the participants' understanding of the term "gifted;"

- whether or not the Hunter graduates felt that having a high IQ had had an appreciable effect on their lives;
- whether or not the participants experienced feeling different from others as a result of being identified as gifted;
- whether or not the participants felt they had achieved personal satisfaction with their life outcomes;
- whether or not the Hunter graduates felt they had lived up to society's expectations concerning their achievement.

We are endeavoring in this book to convey the thoughts and feelings of the high-IQ child as he or she reflects upon that experience later in life. There were, for most of our participants, important advantages to their Hunter education, as well as serious liabilities. For example, the school stringently avoided channeling students into narrow talent areas (except in the case of a few prodigies) or "bookish" behavior, enticing them instead with a broadly enriched curriculum (Hildreth, 1952). Progressive teaching methods incorporating a discovery approach were encouraged by the administration, and rote drill was avoided when possible. Homework was not to be assigned until 5th grade so that students might pursue independent projects.

The people who speak in these pages were among the brightest children in New York City during the 1940s and 1950s. They were offered an education that was considered desirable by families of bright children, as evidenced by the number of candidates who had to be turned away because of limited enrollment. Most of the HCES graduates grew up to be successful and productive by conventional standards. To what extent did participants attribute their success to their experience at the school? We believe the Hunter graduates are eloquent in their descriptions, and wherever possible, their experiences are expressed in their own words. Commentary is added in order to define the context of the quotations.

OVERVIEW

Our report on this population of high-IQ children grown up begins in Chapter 2 with the history of the gifted movement up to the establishment of Hunter College Elementary School in 1941. As a context for the commentary provided by the study participants in later chapters, the school is then described retrospectively by teachers and students, as well as by reports written at the time by administrators and researchers.

Chapter 3 explores the students' responses to being labeled gifted.

Some of the graduates were comfortable with the term; it fit nicely into their developing self-concept. Others found it a source of unbearable expectation, communicated by adults inside and outside of school. These two perspectives (as well as remarks that are less polarized) are reported in the words of the individuals themselves. Being segregated from other children, often requiring a long bus ride out of the local community, exaggerated some of the graduates' feelings of separation from siblings and neighborhood friends. Chapter 3 elaborates on whether or not this sense of difference persisted throughout their lives. Did they view their lives as distinct from those of their families, friends, colleagues, and the "person on the street?"

What kind of family would send a child to a laboratory school for gifted children? The concept of gifted education was not as widespread in the 1940s and 1950s as it is now. Most graduates in this study came from homes where the father was a professional and middle-class values were espoused. Chapter 4 reports the former Hunter students' impressions of the value system that they brought with them to school from their families.

A paradoxical outcome of our interviews was the widely diverse impressions the participants had of the competitive atmosphere of Hunter College Elementary School. In Chapter 5, some Hunter graduates discuss elementary school burnout resulting from pervasive competition. Others enjoyed a supportive, noncompetitive atmosphere. Still others felt dismayed when they entered secondary school with plenty of self-confidence but few traditional learning skills.

We were curious to know whether the women who attended HCES as children in the late 1940s and 1950s remembered experiencing either special attention or sexism. The curriculum seemed to be devoid of overt sex biases and was headed by one of the few existing female administrators. The testimony of the respondents in Chapter 6 reveals pressures that came into play despite the relatively egalitarian elementary school atmosphere.

As mentioned above, by societal standards, this group of adults is relatively successful at midlife in terms of professional accomplishment. However, they have not yet made a significant mark on their respective fields. In Chapter 7 we report the responses to our queries about the quality of life of these individuals, the aspirations to which they held themselves, and how closely they perceived themselves as having met their own or public expectations.

How different is the school today from what it was 40 years ago? Chapter 8 is an overview of the school's current curriculum and admissions process. In the 1990s, the school continues its commitment to providing appropriate educational experiences for intellectually and academically talented children in New York City.

IMPLICATIONS

Although most of our study participants are successful and fairly content with their lives and accomplishments, there are no superstars, no Pulitzer Prize or MacArthur Award winners, and only one or two familiar names. Why? What factors go into producing outstanding individuals? Have the Hunter graduates deliberately chosen to avoid "stardom?" Or did they lack the "right stuff?" Is it possible to identify and nurture truly revolutionary thinkers, those who will go on to transform their fields? Should the role of gifted education be to nurture selected geniuses, or to prepare a larger group of more generalized professionals who contribute in a less spectacular way but in greater numbers? Chapter 9 serves as a summary of the previous chapters and a discussion of the implications of the study for the practice of gifted education. What should be the purposes of special education for high-IQ children? How early, if at all, should exceptional children be channeled into talent areas? If our purpose as special educators is to provide a safe and stimulating environment for children who show potential for rapid and deep intellectual stimulation, our methods should reflect that. If we are interested in talent development, our schools must consider a vast restructuring of both identification and practice. We provide discussion and argument in support of both sides of this issue.

ADDITIONAL READINGS ON
IQ TESTING CONTROVERSY

Alvino, J., McDonnel, R.C., & Richert, S. (1981). National survey of identification practices in gifted and talented education. *Exceptional Children, 48* (2), 124–132.

Baird, L.L. (1985). Do grades and tests predict adult accomplishment? *Research in Higher Education, 23*(1), 3–85.

Chapman, P.D. (1988). *Schools as sorters: Lewis Terman, applied psychology, and the intelligence testing movement, 1890–1930.* New York: New York University Press.

Fancher, R.E. (1985). *The intelligence men: Makers of the IQ controversy.* New York: W.W. Norton.

Feldman, D. (1984). A follow-up of subjects scoring above 180 IQ in Terman's "Genetic Studies of Genius." *Exceptional Children, 50*(6), 518–523.

Gardner, H. (1983). *Frames of mind: The theory of multiple intelligences.* New York: Basic Books.

Gould, S.J. (1981). *The mismeasure of man.* New York: W.W. Norton.

Kamphaus, R.W., & Reynolds, C.R. (1984). Development and structure of the Kaufman Assessment Battery for Children. *Journal of Special Education, 18*(3), 213–228.

Oakes, J. (1985). *Keeping track: How schools structure inequality.* New Haven, CT: Yale University Press.

Pegnato, C.W., & Birch, J.W. (1959). Locating gifted children in junior high school. *Exceptional Children, 25*(7), 300–304.

Rosenbaum, J. (1975). The stratification of the socialization process. *American Sociological Review, 40,* 48–54.

Sears, P., & Barbee, A. (1977). Career and life satisfactions among Terman's gifted women. In J. Stanley, W. George, & C. Solano (Eds.), *The gifted and the creative: A fifty-year perspective* (pp. 28–65). Baltimore, MD: Johns Hopkins University Press.

Silverman, L.K. (Ed.) (1986). Special issue: The IQ controversy. *Roeper Review, 8*(3), 136–206.

Sternberg, R. (1982). Lies we live by: Misapplication of tests in identifying the gifted. *Gifted Child Quarterly, 26,* 63–67.

chapter 2
A Brief Survey of Education for Gifted Children: Setting the Historical Context for Hunter College Elementary School

SIR FRANCIS GALTON: GENIUS STUDYING GENIUS

The British scientist Sir Francis Galton (1822–1911) was among the first to empirically examine the nature of talent. He took a keen interest in the work of his cousin Charles Darwin and began to ponder questions regarding the distribution of human intelligence. Darwin's findings, according to Galton in his work *Memories of My Life* (Galton, 1908, p. 287), produced "a marked epoch in my own mental development as it did in that of human thought generally" (quoted in Forrest, 1974, p. 84).

Galton, who used his coined term "eugenics" in connection with his studies of physical and behavioral traits believed to be inherited, is credited with developing the early principles of psychological testing. As a student at Cambridge he made the observation that academic prowess apparently ran in families. His work *Hereditary Genius* (1869) focused on subjects of exceptionally high mental ability. Based upon the data gathered on these individuals, Galton identified a set of criteria defining eminence, a quality of achievement that society recognizes as culturally valuable, and calculated that roughly 1 in 400 fit into this category.

Following the lineage of 286 judges, Galton found that 1 in 9 qualified as having been either a father, son, or brother of a jurist. Furthermore, bishops, poets, physicians, and novelists who were related to judges were much more likely to inherit the characteristics that assure eminence: intelligence, capacity, zeal, and the motivation to excel in their chosen profession. In response to these observations Galton was complimented by Charles Darwin:

> I do not think I ever, in all my life, read anything more interesting and original—and how well and clearly you put every point…you have made a convert of an opponent in one sense, for I have always maintained that excepting fools, men did not differ much in intellect, only in zeal and hard work. (C. Darwin to F. Galton, December 3, 1869, *Memories of My Life*, p. 290, quoted in Forrest, 1974, p. 101)

Galton's efforts, although methodologically flawed in ignoring the contribution of socioeconomic status, added to the understanding of heredity as a factor in human intelligence. Scientists who committed themselves to this theory diverted the appropriate recognition of environmental influences on a child's learning potential for nearly a century.

ALFRED BINET'S ROLE—TESTS TO DETERMINE INTELLIGENCE

Alfred Binet, with the assistance of his student Theodore Simon, developed the first IQ tests. Binet, director of the psychology laboratory at The Sorbonne, began his studies by examining the data of Paul Broca, who had concluded that the size of an individual's cranium was correlated with his or her level of intellect. By 1904, Binet found enough inconsistencies in this theory to terminate his exploration of physiological factors in human intelligence.

Reasoning was the faculty on which Binet concentrated his studies, constructing tasks to assess cognition in its various aspects. Concurrently, the minister of public education enlisted Binet to identify students who might be unable to keep up with their peers in an ordinary classroom setting, with the aim of providing a specialized education for them. Binet devised a series of tasks like counting, evaluating beauty, and rapid dotting of a page, which would involve basic reasoning processes such as sequencing, comprehension, invention, and evaluation. The test employed a potpourri of skills to assess the general potential of the individual.

The original 1905 version arranged tasks in "an ascending order of difficulty." The next version, published in 1908, "established the criteria used in measuring the so-called IQ ever since" (Gould, 1981, p. 149). The concept of mental age was defined as "the last task a child of normal intelligence should be able to complete successfully" (Gould, 1981 p. 149). Binet, by assigning age levels to each task, then determined IQ by comparing mental age with chronological age. By testing for deficits in cognition, Binet laid the foundation upon which countless students would be categorized and placed within the educational system.

Alfred Binet sustained the belief that his scales were solely designed for the purpose of identifying a group so that its members could be helped by receiving specialized education. He described his tests as "a rough empirical guide, constructed for a limited practical purpose," (Gould, 1981, p. 151), and realized that too many variables were at play to label IQ as an absolute measure of intelligence. Binet would not exclude a child from the benefit of education, no matter how unpromising that person's capacity for learning. He recommended tailoring the curriculum to the student, the inception of smaller classes, and the need to motivate. He also concocted mental gymnastics designed to help students improve their skills, using speed and attention to perform feats of varying difficulty. Binet probably would have been discouraged had he dreamt that his assignment of labeling slow learners would result in a movement that discounted many of his concerns about the potential for improvement.

LEWIS TERMAN AND THE
STANFORD-BINET TESTS

The impact of the tidal wave of immigration from 1890–1917 increased the American school population by over 50%, and increased school costs by over 300% (Chapman, 1988, p. 41). Too many children failed, suffering under the burden of an overcrowded system. A study conducted by Leonard Ayres in 1909 titled *Laggards in our Schools* pointed to the fact that about one third of the students were underachieving as evidence that a large degree of retardation existed among New York City's school population. Girls generally completed elementary school, while boys, apparently to help their families by obtaining employment, dropped out sooner. In addition, many families were transient, further burdening the resources of the schools that received the new students.

Lewis Terman was introduced to Binet's work on measuring mental capacity while completing his Ph.D. at Clark University. Terman was studying under E.H. Lindley, who in turn had been a student of E. Stanley Hall, one of the pioneers of educational testing along with Binet, Galton, Wundt, and Cattell. Eventually appointed Professor of Child Studies at Los Angeles Normal school (later to evolve into U.C.L.A.), Terman pursued the testing of 400 students, who, like Binet's subjects, appeared unable to learn under normal conditions. At this stage, Terman realized the efficacy of using Binet's latest test for children of all mental levels, to deliver "a more reliable and more enlightening estimate of the child's intelligence than most teachers can offer after a year of daily contact in the classroom" (Chapman, 1988, p. 26). His proposal was motivated by the fact that many overage students continued to swell the schools. Terman's studies led him to believe that students of varying abilities should be grouped homogeneously.

Soon after moving to Stanford University, Terman produced his first revision of Binet's test, naming it the Stanford-Binet Test. He extended the scale downward to the age of 5 and upward to 16, asserting that his "test constituted a valid measure of intelligence, that the IQ was constant, and that it was greatly influenced by heredity" (Chapman, 1988, p. 28). These beliefs stirred some controversy, because age, home environment, or the presence and quality of school instruction were not taken into account. Also, the normal sample he used was comprised mostly of middle-class, native-born Caucasians. The new science of psychology questioned the art of measuring intellect, but Terman received enough support from influential colleagues at Stanford to introduce his scale into the national educational system.

Another influx of immigrants reached the United States following World War I, providing further impetus for scientists and educators to perfect instruments by which they could group students with their intellectual peers. Terman's tests were employed to channel large groups of new students into the American education system. In 1922, Terman suggested a multitrack plan providing for five groups: gifted, bright, average, slow, and special. Those in the higher strata would be steered toward college preparatory curricula; others would pursue a vocational future or be graduated with a general diploma. Terman dismissed the belief that there existed "the infinite capacity of education to improve social opportunity" (Chapman, 1988, p. 92), remaining convinced that the dull would never climb out of this category, and that the superior would always remain superior. However, cognizant of the politics surrounding a notion of fixed judgments, Terman advocated keeping open "the road for transfers from track to track" (Terman, 1922, p. 19). However, most students directed into one of the five groups tended to maintain their status.

Spurred on by early efforts in the testing of gifted students, Terman, in 1921, began in-depth studies of approximately 1,500 upper elementary grade California children with IQs of 140 and above. The variables of interest were sex ratio, anthropometric measurements, racial origins, school progress, health and physical history, personality and character traits, specialized abilities, and intellectual, social, and play interests. The subjects were identified at approximately age 10 as intellectually gifted (Stanford-Binet IQ of 140 +), and were then (and still are) followed over the course of their lifetimes (Sears, 1977; Tomlinson-Keasey & Little, 1990), in order to test two major hypotheses: first, that advanced intellectual development does not imply social maladjustment; and second, that early identification of intellectual ability can be a fairly accurate predictor of adult productivity and success.

In 1950, Terman and his associates conducted the third follow-up study of the original subject group at midlife (Terman & Oden, 1959). By middle age, most of these gifted children had indeed grown up to be relatively well-adjusted, productive adults. Yet Terman's study has been criticized because of the restricted socioeconomic, geographical, and historical range of the sample. A disproportionate number of the 1,528 subjects came from homes in which the father was a professional, and virtually all lived in the Los Angeles and San Francisco Bay areas (Sears, 1984). Finally, the study participants experienced the Great Depression as part of their early adulthood.

By today's standards, the Terman midlife questionnaire (Terman & Oden, 1959), adapted for use in the present study, was poorly designed. The coding schemes are awkward to use, and the language used to define the end point of rating scales is in some places so convoluted as to obfuscate the definition of the variable under study. Terman's fascination with health and genetic issues led him to focus inordinate attention on physical health and the mental acuity of subjects' children, while underemphasizing other areas such as motivational and environmental influences on career and personal success. The questionnaire did, however, incorporate over 100 variables, including occupation, marital, personality, and political factors, as well as items concerning life satisfaction and factors that supported or obstructed accomplishment.

In 1922, Terman was elected president of the American Psychological Association. In a lecture delivered at his inauguration, he defined characteristics of the highly gifted: "in general, appreciably superior to unselected children in physique, health and social adjustment;

markedly superior in moral attitudes as measured by character tests or trait ratings; and vastly superior in their mastery of school subjects" (Barbe & Renzulli, 1981, p. 8). Following the publication of Terman's follow-up reports in 1945 and 1955, many others undertook the examination of optimal facilities for the gifted, including rapid advancement through school.

EXPERIMENTAL SCHOOLS FOR THE GIFTED

Education of the gifted in the United States began over a century ago with rapid acceleration as the method of choice. The Cambridge Plan (1893) provided parallel sections in each class, covering material in different time spans. Track systems, winnowing out the gifted from the general school population, and accelerating the time in which it took to teach the curriculum, were established in Elizabeth, New Jersey; Batavia, New York; Detroit, Michigan; and Santa Barbara, California. Rapid advancement programs also were begun in Worcester, Massachusetts and New York City.

The concept of individualized instruction proposed in 1912 by Frederick Burk became the forerunner of other programs designed exclusively for the gifted. Most notable was "The Winnetka Plan," instituted in 1919, which subdivided the traditional curriculum into contract units which the student undertook to complete in a given time. The plan went a step beyond other progressive educational techniques by calling for cooperation among students. Prominent schools designed to educate the gifted were the Cook County Normal School (1883), the Horace Mann School (1887), the Speyer School (1899), the State University of Iowa Experimental School (1915), and the Lincoln School of Teachers College, Columbia University (1917) (Columbia Encyclopedia, 1956, p. 1603).

The Los Angeles, California; Rochester, New York; and Cleveland, Ohio educational systems organized "opportunity classes" in 1918 in order to separate the brightest grade-school students from their slower learning counterparts. By 1925, special classes for gifted learners were cropping up all over the nation. At this time, class performance, teacher judgment, and standardized testing formed the basis for placement of students in these programs. Educators Gary Whipple, T.S. Henry, H.T. Manuel, and Genevieve Coy conducted studies of special aptitudes for certain disciplines, like music and drawing. In 1922, at an annual meeting of the National Society for the Study of Education, some leading figures in the field of testing, including Edward L. Thorndike, met to analyze the history and administrative use of intelligence testing (Chapman, 1988, p. 165). The question of using these IQ tests nationwide was debated. The proponents raised the issue of producing a more scientific education that would prove efficient at conserving talent. The opponents of this enterprise brought up the possibility of misusing test scores, thus placing some students at a disadvantage (Chapman, 1988, p. 165).

Leta Hollingworth and Jacob Theobald, the latter the principal of Public School (P.S.) 165 in Manhattan, in 1922–1923, initiated a project whose goal was to carry on an intensive study of the gifted. Concurrently, a Teachers College course on the education of gifted children was offered by Hollingworth (Hildreth, 1966, p. 50). At P.S. 55, the Speyer School provided an experimental site that set the stage for a 1935 Board of Education policy providing special classes for the gifted. The Terman classes, in recognition of Lewis M. Terman, were designed around a course of study inspired by Hollingworth's belief that "high ability students should be provided with an educational program that promotes both cognitive and affective development" (White & Renzulli, 1987, p. 89). Despite Terman's support for rapid advancement through the school curriculum, enrichment rather than acceleration was the key philosophy practiced and advocated.

Honors classes, special classes in foreign languages, and other extracurricular programs were offered to gifted learners in the 1930s in the secondary schools. In various parts of the nation, special schools were established exclusively for gifted learners. These were situated in big cities with large concentrations of students from which could be drawn the most intellectually able. During the Great Depression, enrichment, rather than acceleration, became the recommended method of administering to the gifted because of the dearth of job opportunities awaiting high school and college graduates.

Early identification was cited as one of the most important factors necessary for children of prodigious mental capacity. Offering a diversity of courses enriched in depth and breadth to meet the needs of these special children was also mentioned as being particularly valuable. Hollingworth recognized that "a gifted child may be far more excellent in some capacities than in others" and "may even fall below the average in certain capacities" (1926, p. 202, quoted in Tannenbaum, 1983, p. 7).

Influenced by the work of Leta Hollingworth, Hunter College established a model school in 1941 to serve high-IQ students from nursery school to grade six. Before that time, Hunter College administered a model elementary school to serve as a teacher training center for its undergraduates. Hollingworth's experiments demonstrated that high-IQ children present special challenges to teachers, administrators, and to themselves. To a large degree, the success or failure of such students later in life was believed to be contingent upon their early education: the earlier the recognition and tailoring of special programs for the gifted, the better. The most well-adjusted high IQ students were expected to be those who were educated with their intellectual peers.

HUNTER COLLEGE ELEMENTARY SCHOOL: 1940–1960

Hunter College Elementary School initiated its new policy as a school for the intellectually gifted in 1941, replacing its function as a model school for nonspecifically selected students. Precedent had been set first at P.S. 165, and then at P.S. 500's Speyer School under the direction of Leta Hollingworth. At Hunter, high-IQ children residing within specified geographical parameters (including most of Manhattan) were solicited, screened, and selected. Three floors of a wing of Hunter College's new Park Avenue building situated between Lexington and Park Avenues and 68th Street were allocated to the new school. Within minutes of the finest museums, art galleries, libraries, and theaters, Hunter's high-rise campus held promise for its newest clients as a facility that offered better and more numerous cultural resources than perhaps any other in the world. Results from the Speyer School experiment had supported the premise that when enrolled among their peers, gifted children fulfilled their predicted academic potential. It seemed prudent to continue to explore methods of enhancing the education of high-IQ children in a setting that would ensure optimum benefit to those who took an interest in this specialty: educators, psychologists, and counselors.

The first group of Hunter's gifted young pupils entered the school during 1941. By 1947, the last of the unselected students had either been graduated or had transferred to another school. Underwritten by the Board of Higher Education, Hunter's campus school was open to students from the ages of 3 to 11. Funding was first guaranteed for a period of seven years, but extensions have continued to the present, and the school, now located on East 94th Street, remains a laboratory in which studies of the development and education of intellectually gifted children are conducted.

Admission Standards

Requirements for admission to Hunter's campus school were so stringent that it earned a reputation as one of the most highly selective grade schools in the nation. While hundreds applied, fewer than 60 were admitted each year. Pupils usually began the application procedure with the recommendation of their teachers in public and private schools. A score of 130 or above on the individually administered 1937 revision of the Stanford-Binet test (Form L-M) was required for entrance. "Applicants must be residents of the borough of Manhattan within the boundary of Washington Heights to the north, 14th Street to the south," wrote Hildreth, in *Educating Gifted Children At Hunter College Elementary School* (1952, p. 20). Although such geographic restrictions eliminated from consideration students who resided outside these bounds, according to alumni interviewed for this study, knowledgeable parents found ways of circumventing the rules.

The second screening involved detailed observation and interviews with parent and child. A committee on admissions evaluated each applicant and made the final decision. At the beginning, and for many years afterward, high-IQ siblings of enrolled students were granted preference for admission, and roughly equal gender composition was sought.

Headed by a principal and assisted by a clerk registrar and advisors from the campus school committee, Hunter College Elementary School offered an enriched curriculum in the form of courses in art and music appreciation, studio art, science, and foreign language (French and German). A director of research studies coordinated the campus school with the college. The 22 classrooms were built to conform to the most modern design of the times. Features included movable furniture to encourage freedom of mobility, in-class sinks, built-in cabinets and cloak rooms, easels, workbenches, large bulletin boards, a bountifully equipped library, a small theater, and a large open-air terrace for exercise or free play. (More details are presented in Appendix B, "Physical Conditions.") The students brought lunch from home and had access to the undergraduate cafeteria for beverages. The college assembly hall was available to the children, who also enjoyed the use of a carpentry shop, a greenhouse, a gymnasium, an observatory for weather instruments, and a swimming pool.

Goals and Their Implementation

For the gifted students at Hunter College Elementary School an optimal intellectual experience was paramount, but so were the goals of social adjustment and the development of values that would assure a fruitful and fulfilling future. Although other aims like "the training of leaders in the realms of ideas as well as in the social sphere" (Hildreth, 1952, p. 42) were articulated, it appears that many graduates have, in retrospect, agreed that more than not, assertiveness in exhibiting talents or strengths was not considered a desirable trait. Democracy and fair play were stressed; competitiveness was played down. Former students interviewed for this study remember "coasting along," except for occasional "boning up" for the all-important standardized tests. Many students recall the joy of associating with others on a par intellectually; in fact, the quality of life at Hunter was such that once the students left the environment, it became apparent to them that their experience had been extraordinary and was never to be duplicated. A female homemaker, age 48, stated, "It set me up for disappointment in other schools."

Although Hunter adopted a progressive stance, allowing its students and teachers freedom of mobility and expression along with the privileges of collaborating in the planning and execution of units of study, a certain degree of rigidity, a vestige of the tightly structured traditional system remained (see Appendix B, "Physical Conditions" and Appendix C, "Routine Movements"). While much tolerance for airing opinions and sharing ideas existed, little patience was shown for those who engaged in antisocial behavior. The teacher maintained firm control while giving students freedom to chart their own courses of study and to feel at ease in expressing themselves without fear of being ridiculed for ideas that were new or unusual.

The stated goals of educating gifted children advocated self-actualization, while stressing social responsibility. The fostering of ethical attitudes, free expression, decision-making skills, realistic evaluation of abilities and limitations, and a pursuit of interests and aptitudes (Hildreth, 1952, p. 44) appear similar to those aims articulated by all educators. Certainly, the unusual nature of the school population dictated goals geared toward leadership and achievement, or at least the responsibility of the gifted child to live up to a potential quite unlike any expected of the average pupil. Interestingly, according to some graduates, an atmosphere promoting such goals did not prevail.

An interdisciplinary approach was implemented at the school. Instead of isolating areas of study, teachers integrated subjects so that themes would emerge, allowing the students to recognize relationships among the academic disciplines. Open-ended teaching inevitably enriched the curriculum by permitting those engaged in the process to expand the scope of the lesson. The unit was stressed so that various aspects of a topic would be explored. For example, a geography lesson on Australia evolved into a discussion of the strategic value of the continent and the surrounding islands during World War II. Rather than viewing this as a failure to adhere to the intended scope of the lesson, the instructors were pleased that the class, responding with so much enthusiasm, was motivated to delve more deeply into the subject.

Instructional media were frequently used to enrich a lesson visually or aurally. A unit in science might, for instance, require the production of charts and graphs; a dramatic or musical recital could evolve from the same lesson; perhaps a field trip, a creative writing exercise, or even a mathematical problem and its solution might have been used to bring a point across. Built into the daily activities was a planning session in which the student might construct a unit of study and suggest the various disciplines and activities related to the broad topic. There existed something for everyone, a smorgasbord of subjects from which a student could select his or her favorite area of concentration.

Such enrichment of curricula was thought to preclude the need to accelerate individual children at Hunter's campus school, although occasionally a child would be skipped in the very early grades. Such solutions had traditionally been employed in other school systems where a student was clearly performing far ahead of his or her age-grade norm. The assertion of educators like Gertrude Hildreth, Florence Brumbaugh, and Frank Wilson, all outstanding advocates of the highly gifted child, was that acceleration robbed these children of time vital for developmental learning in the grade school years. The acquisition of strategic processes, they maintained, might be lost if a child were pushed ahead, and such gaps might not be manifested until a later stage. Moreover, these educators felt that social adjustment to an older group would present a disadvantage to a gifted child (Hildreth, 1952, pp. 259–261). Given that all the children at Hunter were talented intellectually, they could be accelerated and enriched while maintaining an age-appropriate peer group.

A policy statement issued by the school describes how the administration viewed itself in light of its aims to provide an appropriate educational experience for its special charges:

> The awareness of the complexities of giftedness encourages our staff to provide highly diversified classroom activities and modes of operation which differ from the conventional. Varied activities, varied choices and materials, encouragement of pupil planning, initiative and originality are reflective of our school where each gifted child is recognized as an individual.... An open, flexible school environment, a blending of openness and structure, and above all, respect for the individual.... They are encouraged to be involved in independent activities...they need the opportunity to learn at their own pace...to use and expand their skills in dealing with significant questions and issues and with experimentation and exploration of content. (Unpublished and undated manuscript in Hunter College Campus Schools Archives)

The term "competition" does not appear in this policy paper, although it implies that students were encouraged to proceed at their own pace and to follow their own interests and pursuits to achieve optimum results. Respondents often recalled that Hunter provided a highly nurturing environment. According to a 39-year-old banker:

> Because classes were small, the pupils received a lot of individual attention. We did do things like French in third grade which is nowadays pretty commonplace, but it wasn't in 1955.

A 38-year-old executive observed that

> The school had a very progressive outlook in the way that it treated students. Incredible friendships were formed. It was a very humane environment that was cultivated by the teachers, the opportunities they provided.

Many students cherished freedom of expression and movement as a quality unique to the campus school. The executive cited above speaks of

> an open type of setting...a teacher who would put on a radio or record at lunch time and we'd dance in the classroom...boys and girls together, which was really quite something...very open, very friendly.

The teachers of the gifted sought to instill in their pupils such admirable traits as trustworthiness, teamwork, self-control, and sharing; however, such goals were hardly the exclusive province of gifted education. Discipline problems did not exist to the extent found in mainstream schools; a white card was issued to those who misbehaved, and a visit to the principal sufficed as punishment in these cases. One student remembered "being in tears" because he was under the impression that earning five white cards meant explusion (which was not the case). An experienced teacher could often prevent discord among the lively students and maintain harmony by application of sound educational principles such as enlisting the cooperation of these pupils in helping one another (see Appendix C, "Routine Movements").

Students in grade two (ages 6–7) and above had nine activity slots daily, provided field trips and other special events did not intrude. Such activities and subjects as planning (collaboration between teacher and students on contents and applications of lessons), mathematics, and science lab were arranged for half the class. The others received instruction in music, language arts, or citizenship; had their lunch; or participated in group reading, creative expression, or outdoor play. Enrichment through special activities like foreign language, audiovisual resources, arts and handicrafts, library, and special interest clubs including chess, camera, stamps and coins, dramatics, musical recorder, and model building, drew many interested students. Although the New York City public schools offered several of these enrichment options, they generally lacked the foreign language, audiovisual resources, and special interest clubs.

Curricular goals stressed both depth and breadth of knowledge. Themes or units of study assured that topics in the social studies and sciences encompassed a wide range of skills and activities. Often, lessons surpassed their scope and crossed over into a secondary-school level. If a particular subject hit a responsive chord among the students, a lively and stimulating lesson would result. The knowledge some of these 'experts' had acquired through their reading and, in many cases, travels, enriched the curriculum and gave rise to topics that spanned broad areas and spawned the pursuit of independent research and writing.

Skills were taught and exercised through workbook drill, but some students complained that they did not master all the basics and that the school took for granted their ability to learn quickly and easily. A 46-year-old graduate remarked that "Hunter didn't prepare me at all in aspects of report writing or story writing." A female graduate regretted that "I didn't feel that I had a good background in rote." Instruction was lax "in foundation skills."

"You don't need that stuff because you're intellectually gifted; let's do interesting things," is how one former student paraphrased the prevailing attitude. His reaction was:

> It's nice to be smart, but that doesn't go very far. If you don't have self-discipline and motivation, and you don't know how to work, and you don't know how to study, and you don't know how to organize your time, it doesn't go very far.

Despite these assessments by some, many more expressed feelings akin to those of a college professor, age 48, who valued "having been allowed and encouraged to learn freely and with excitement; never being held back....I really appreciated being given materials that excited me."

Most Hunter children did not have to wait for the remainder of the class to catch up. The students were grouped according to ability in reading and mathematics. One class, in fact, had three reading groups, "Phi," "Beta," and "Kappa," a not-too-subtle effort by the instructor to inspire her charges to aim for excellence.

Quite a number of respondents recall encountering difficulty with a particular subject despite their being labeled as academically talented. One graduate admitted to "lacking basic skills like spelling," and another spoke of math as being "a source of absolute panic, dismay, and agony." It was not uncommon for a student teacher to be assigned to work one-on-one with a student to help him or her over difficulties. Those students who skipped one of the early grades recall having to catch up to their older classmates. One of the most positive effects of the relatively small classes and high level of personal interest evinced by the teachers toward their students was that of support for those pupils who encountered difficulty in mastering those skills or concepts that were taught. It appears that the children were nurtured, protected, and even insulated in their early educational experience. This pattern may have facilitated learning and growth, but for some it caused a rude awakening once they emerged into the reality of secondary school.

Because Hunter was designated an experimental school, innovation was encouraged, and new methods of teaching tested. Educators of the gifted and other interested persons often visited the school and observed these "super-learners." The children, aware that they were in a special school and accustomed to frequent testing and scrutiny, were not at all self-conscious with strangers in the classroom and did not particularly "play" to the audience. Nevertheless, many respondents recall valuing "that special feeling that we all felt cared for."

A 48-year-old graduate related an anecdote in which

> A woman was visiting the class. I was called up to explain how to get to a certain place...I belatedly realized that this wasn't about the woman getting to the bus stop; it was about me giving directions.

Although between three and four decades have passed since the respondents attended Hunter College Elementary School, what they now value most about the experience offers revealing glimpses of the educational experiment they shared.

> I was never bored there. (Female, age 47)

> I subsequently saw my children grow up in a regular public school environment. I saw individuality and humor being squelched. That was never done to any of us. (Female, age 48)

> It was always interesting, always fascinating...it made me feel very positive about school. (Male, age 50)

> Hunter was a very positive experience for me and I'm glad it existed. It's too bad that there's such fierce competition to get in there....I think that in some very important ways, I am who I am because of Hunter. I value the support and encouragement and respect from the environment. (Male, age 41)

I remember a sense of excitement about learning...teachers that were tremendously involved with us as students...an exciting student body, and a sense that that was where I wanted to be every morning. (Female, age 48)

Because one of the major goals of the school was to provide on-the-job training for undergraduates of the college who wished to pursue a career in teaching, it was the duty of the primary instructor to establish a role model for the student teacher. Many teachers and student teachers were enthusiastic mentors; nevertheless, quite a few former students harbored negative feelings. Some respondents mentioned gaps in their education and the failure of the school to teach the basic or fundamentals.

A male musician, age 39, stated:

There was almost no counseling of any type. There was pressure. I didn't have good work habits...I didn't develop good work habits in school. No one seemed to take a particular interest in it.

From a female banker, age 39:

There was very little homework. It was more of an emphasis on developing the intellect. I think they were a little too hung up on the intellectually gifted concept—as though if you made it through your biennial IQ test, then don't worry about it. In fact, most students were so frequently tested that it became second nature to face such challenges.

The Teachers

The teachers were very interested in teaching and in us. They were highly motivated...aware that they were in a special program and proud of it...excited by it.

The opinion of this female banker is shared by many of the former students of the school. Ideally, teachers of the gifted had to be screened carefully to assure that they would meet the needs of these special students. The dual responsibility of training future teachers and molding "superior" minds made it incumbent upon the primary teacher to possess qualities above and beyond those of a teacher of unselected pupils. To prevent the misfortune of educational mismatches (i.e., students who proved too challenging for their mentors), the main requirement dictated that the effective teacher be gifted, imaginative, resourceful, and inspirational (Hildreth, 1952). In addition, teachers of the gifted had to be ingenious, for the breadth and depth of knowledge and ability required of them were limitless. At any time, a student could pose a question that might challenge or stump the teacher. Although it would be no disgrace for the teacher to suggest that occasionally the inquirer find the answer on his or her own, it would not have been suitable to routinely offer this solution.

The Hunter teachers were probably a microcosm of the diverse personalities staffing schools all over the nation. Some teachers were casually self-assured and led gently but with persistence, while others had to exercise rigid control to contain the often effervescent and irrepressible students.

The teacher of the gifted who possessed a rich cultural heritage was valued, as well as one with a good sense of humor, a positive trait frequently found in exceptionally gifted children (Hildreth, 1952). A sense of fairness, a healthy outlook on life, and skills and accomplishments in various areas were also assets.

A female writer, age 48, mentioned

an outstanding teacher whom I was fortunate enough to have for two years...very dynamic. She had been a WAC [Women's Army Corps]. I think that showed somehow. None of us forgot the 'Dance of the Decimal' by which we learned decimals...Others...were as much of interest by being characters as by being so outstanding.

According to another graduate, the science teacher played a significant role in his life.

My first look into a microscope...[was a] very influential thing in many ways supporting my original decision early on to go into medicine.

The prospective teacher of the gifted was to have achieved an outstanding track record in his or her profession and, above all, scholarship in the learning process. This person was expected to be familiar with the principles of child psychology and to possess that intangible but vital ingredient: an instinct for dealing with children and bringing out their best qualities. The recollections of Teacher M (see Appendix D) highlight some of the specialized instruction given to those selected to teach at the school and reveal a keen sensitivity and recognition of the needs of the exceptionally gifted child. Some memorable teachers emerged, and they are still influencing their former students 30 years later.

A female program specialist was impressed with Audio-Visual Education.

I picked up an appreciation of art...today I absolutely love museums and paintings...that was the best program I had at Hunter.

Many of the respondents reacted to their teachers as a group in a similar manner to a female college professor, 48, who remembered "with great fondness" some of her teachers.

I had the feeling…that they really loved us. Many of the teachers were wonderful. For the most part, they were with us and encouraged us. I loved being there.

In principle, teachers were expected to conform to the standards set by the committee that hired them, and to fulfill the educational directives; however, not all were well-suited to their professions. Some of the graduates singled out specific teachers who demonstrated negative qualities.

One alumna recalls an unusual form of discipline used at Hunter at the time.

If you were bad, you had to sit in the bathroom. They would move your desk into the bathroom for hours.

A former Hunter student, age 40, spoke of a "fruitcake," a teacher who put her through "a terrible experience" by making an example of her in front of the entire class because her notebook was "the worst in the whole class." A female graduate, age 48, remembered "one who was a very difficult and unpleasant person who would scream at us, 'The audacity of you!'….I remember not knowing what 'audacity' meant."

Student teachers from Hunter College who were assigned to the elementary school (usually for a period of six weeks, either during the morning or afternoon) could not fail to notice the contrast between the Hunter children and those of the public schools. It was considered a privilege to be a student teacher at Hunter. The children were, in the majority of cases, willing subjects who made it easy for teachers to be at their best. The elementary school pupils at Hunter, often sensing the vulnerability of the student teachers, were more than willing to cooperate to make them look good. Not quite authority figures, the student teachers, if they were reasonably responsive to the children's needs, could win their confidence, and often their affection. Perceived as one to whom respect was due, yet one who might be more understanding and amenable to demands than the primary teacher, the undergraduate teacher straddled two worlds: he or she was a friend cum mentor. Attachments between pupils and students teachers often took root, and the children frequently curried the favor of their teachers-in-training. At times, a group assigned to the student teacher would jockey for position; capturing the attention of the teacher was the goal. Good-natured, but occasionally serious rivalries among the children sometimes escalated into verbal matches. Showing off by the pupil, while hardly accepted by the primary teacher, was tolerated by the uninitiated student teacher who, at times, was bewildered by the liveliness and ingenuity of her charges. When the time arrived for the student teacher to rotate to another class or school, the students were often upset. "Let's barricade the door," and "those lucky ducks," referring to the next class to be instructed by a departing student teacher, were expressions of the students' regret that they were losing someone with whom they had formed a special, albeit short-lived, attachment. Such was the intensity of these relationships that to this day, some children remember their student teachers and vice versa.

The Students

Owing to the efforts of Leta Hollingworth and Louis Terman, a composite picture of high-IQ children emerged: They were remarkable in a variety of characteristics, both physical and intellectual. Many enjoyed fine health and a diversity of interests, were personable and charming, knew how to get along with others, and were inquisitive and alert.

To the uninitiated visitor, the overwhelming impression the Hunter College Elementary School student body created was not that of encountering a race of superkids, but rather of being among confident, demonstrative, well-behaved students who asserted their individual qualities to an extent surpassing the average pupil. The children seemed comfortable with themselves and each other; though some were apparently loners, most gravitated toward a group. A sizable number of pupils enjoyed a high socioeconomic status, and some had parents who were eminent and even celebrated. Others, who categorized themselves as belonging to a predominantly liberal lower-middle or solidly middle class, were clearly aware of these distinctions among their peers.

A male psychologist, age 44, mentioned

an economic background that was lower-middle class, although culturally it was on a par with that of my classmates....I always felt somewhat self-conscious about not being as well-dressed or thinking of myself not being able to afford things that the other kids had....A lot of the kids were really affluent upper-middle-class Jewish kids who were, like myself, somewhat ethnocentric about life, which would not have been the case and was not the case once I returned to mainstream public school.

Generally, the Hunter children dressed casually, sometimes reflecting a lifestyle not usually enjoyed by the typical public school student. For instance, several times a week certain children wore jodhpurs to class so that they could go directly from school to their horseback-riding lessons. In the 1940s and 1950s, students in the public schools often had to adhere to a standard dress code of dresses or skirts for girls and shirts and ties for boys.

A typical school day provided ample stimulation for most students who in turn exhibited an eagerness for learning. Willing and able, they often rewarded the primary instructor or student teacher with enthusiasm and acceptance. While some pupils were quiet and did not insinuate their presence upon others, many enjoyed the limelight. The trick was to allow that student his or her place in the sun while not denying others their fair share of attention. One teacher advised a student frustrated at being misunderstood to "suffer fools gladly," a phrase Leta Hollingworth frequently quoted from St. Paul's epistle (Corinthians II, 11:19) "For ye suffer fools gladly, seeing ye yourselves are wise." Whether this attitude fostered elitism or merely satisfied a frustration, it is clear that a few children were learning to accommodate to a world not in sync with their own.

Judging from the responses of the former students, it is apparent that the intimate sharing of experiences with others of like ability and interests formed a core of deep satisfaction among the children. A female historian, age 46, considered her years at Hunter

> the most beneficial experience. It was probably like going to Harvard when you're three. It's the other students. It was fantastic.

Despite the lofty goals set forth by the administration and the largely positive memories expressed by many respondents, there remained pockets of discontent about the philosophies, curricula, and teachers that painted a more critically reflective picture of HCES.

chapter 3
On Being Labeled Gifted

Recalling their years at Hunter College Elementary School, the respondents of this study considered the nature of their being labeled gifted. Before considering their remarks, we should emphasize that up to the launch of Sputnik in 1957, intellectual giftedness was defined primarily in terms of IQ and academic achievement. Parents or teachers would recommend potential students of Hunter College Elementary School for testing with an individual aptitude instrument. The children were thus identified on the basis of IQ at or above the 97th percentile on the L-M form of the Stanford-Binet. Supporting information, including an interview with the child that explored verbal and behavioral maturity, completed the admission process.

Some cited as evidence of their giftedness precocity and academic achievement far above their mainstream peers. Many, however, were skeptical about the weight and validity of IQ tests as indicators of intellectual ability.

I think that scoring high on a test has nothing to do with the real world, and therefore, I don't think that I ever would consider myself gifted based on how I performed on a test. (Female, age 43)

You can't worship an IQ test. I (as an attorney) represent a lot of prisoners who have IQs like 80, yet when there are crucial issues that affect them personally, suddenly they become very smart. As I got older, I realized IQ tests are at least partially your eagerness to perform well and your focal concentration at that moment. (Female, age 46)

I've begun to question the whole notion of IQ, certainly the traditional verbal/quantitative system of measuring IQ. I like some of the work that

Gardner or Sternberg are doing. I think there's a far broader range of what intelligence is. I'm lousy spatially and can't drive worth a damn. I'm not musical, and I think these are all aspects of intelligence.

Some of the Stanford-Binet Hunter system of IQ measurement, I'm no longer comfortable with. (Female, age 46)

A few, like the screenwriter quoted below, even took exception to the term "gifted." They often suggested that it is highly arbitrary.

'Gifted' has always seemed to me a loaded metaphor. What's the gift exactly? High IQ scores? 'Intelligence?' And who's giving it? The Gods? Is the gift something for the trophy room? The playroom? The office wall? Can it be exchanged if it doesn't fit? 'Gifted child' has, from the get-go, pre-packaged connotations. Just as the words 'Born to Lose' tattooed on your arm as a tot increase the chances you'll grow up to deal drugs for pocket money, the words 'trust fund' etched into your mind raise the odds you'll make the Ivy League and serve on a board of directors. The wealthy don't need to separate their 'gifted children' on the basis of IQ testing; all their kids get special handling, so attendance at a 'special' public school for 'gifted children' tells a child where it doesn't come from and where to go—i.e. into the professions and/or upper-middle class.

Growing up 'identified early in life'—bubble-wrapped in societal-parental expectations/options—so consistently [statistically] shapes kids' 'performance' in later life, it seems as odd to keep proving this as it is to assume that schooling, not [social] class, is the key causal factor. (Female, age 41)

Most agree that high IQ, as ascertained by a standardized test, does not in itself assure that an individual is gifted in any area other than test taking. Mental acuity, according to many, is a much more valid indicator of giftedness. A former student stated:

I have a tendency to see the big picture very quickly, the consequences of things very quickly, and I believe that that is one of the real things about being intelligent: that something happens and you immediately see the tentacles go out, and then, you see the end point.... I just believe it is the ability to see what is going to happen and the ability to see what is going on, to get it all together, to synthesize it, and to know the consequences. And that's hard to live with. (Female, age 41)

I don't recall any particular term used to describe us but we all knew what we were. We all knew that we had high IQs. By the third grade, we knew that an IQ of 100 was normal and had learned how to peek at the records to discover ours. We knew we could outperform other children in intellectual pursuits. How did it feel? Good. I knew I could always win back all the marbles that, because of my poor shooting, I would lose to the neighborhood boys, by talking them into playing poker. I don't think that the high-IQ label had significant effect; the fact would have been apparent without the label. (Male, age 45)

Awareness of being gifted occurs when the child is able to compare himself or herself to peers. For those students who came to Hunter from other schools, recognition of their intellectual prowess came earlier than for those who began their education at Hunter at the earliest grade.

Greenlaw and McIntosh (1988, p. 41), citing Coleman and Fults (1982, pp. 116-120), pointed out that

An interesting phenomenon occurs when gifted students are segregated. Because of a tendency to compare oneself with others in whom there is a perceived similarity, gifted students compare themselves with the other superior student in their homogeneous classroom rather than with their average age mates. Thus, their self-concept may decline when they are first placed in a homogeneous grouping, but it will reascend when their primary reference group is comprised of a heterogeneous mixture.

Consider now what one of our respondents, an editor, said:

I remember feeling way out of touch. I was moved from first grade in a public school to third in Hunter. It may have been a grievous error. I worked to catch up. This set up a negative feeling about school. I assumed I was smart. In my group (in public school) I had been smartest. When I caught up in fifth and sixth grade, there seemed to be a strong emphasis on science. There were two very special students, and it occurred to me that they were a lot smarter than me. I was amazed at how far ahead some were in math and science. (Female, age 40)

A female college professor, age 48, remembers:

I was put in a public school in New Jersey for a couple of weeks. I went immediately to the top of the class; I got stars for everything I did. I took that for granted. At Hunter, I never felt inferior. I was not afraid of any subject till high school where I started having difficulty in math because of a nasty teacher.... Gifted is being able to do whatever better than others. I was aware early on that I was in the top reading group. I guess there was some sort of feeling that some were at the top. I always had a feeling I was up there. It felt natural to be where I was; I did not feel out of place. I don't think I gave it much thought who was or wasn't smart. Some things impressed me. At six or seven, one boy said he wanted to be an ornithologist, and he could spell it.

Greenlaw and McIntosh (1988) asserted:

In general, gifted students' self-concepts are closely tied with their academic learning. Since they usually do well academically, it follows that most gifted students have positive self-concepts. (p. 41)

It does not necessarily follow that because high-IQ children feel good about themselves, they do not require encouragement. Davis and Rimm (1985) noted that researchers have found that compared with nongifted students, a large proportion of gifted students are low in self-esteem. Kanoy, Johnson, and Kanoy (1980), Whitmore (1980), and Terman and Oden (1951), report that underachieving gifted students and adults have lower self-esteem and more negative self-concepts than high-achieving gifted persons. Indeed, these children often need not only to be affirmed in their successes, but also to be motivated to work beyond their capacities so that they might achieve far more than they or others might have expected (Greenlaw & McIntosh, 1988, p. 42).

Respondents attempted to define giftedness in the following ways:

I think giftedness is multi-faceted....I think I have a gift in a certain sense....A lot of teachers and adults tried to tell me that I was gifted because I was good in math. A synthesizing and perceptive sense of elements is my gift. (Male, age 40)

Gifted, of course, is relative....Within my profession, I think I am more talented than most of the lawyers I've dealt with. I think I have more sheer talent. (Male, age 50)

I think there are two meaningful approaches to giftedness. One has simply to do with ability. Hunter, at least when we went there, seemed to identify giftedness solely or almost solely with intellectual potential as measured on IQ tests. That, I assume, is why you found little correlation with artistic achievement. And I think that focus on intellect alone is limiting as an ability-based definition. Clearly, there are other sorts of ability gifts, most obviously in the form of artistic talent. But there's another, and I think more valuable approach to recognizing giftedness, I think, which builds upon ability but doesn't stop there. Massive native intelligence (or performing or production talent, for that matter) only becomes what I would call true giftedness when coupled with a strong imaginative or creative streak. Thus, rather than defining the gifted as merely especially able, we would look for people who challenge, who are inclined to question or to reinvent the world. (Male, age 40)

I have a different definition. I feel that unless I made some kind of real contribution to my field or to the world in general, I guess I'm not sure that I would say I was gifted. (Female, age 39)

There is no one person who is absolutely right. You can read someone who is so definite and sure that this is right and then go to the library and find a book on the same subject by someone who is absolutely sure that he or she is right, and it is 180 degrees different from the first person. Well, anyway, it's being aware of all the differences, and making your own choices, and feeling good about having the confidence to make your own choices. And that, I really feel good about. I think that that's grand. That's what I want to pass on to my children. (Female, age 41)

Others dismissed the idea that they are gifted. Consider these examples:

I didn't consider myself gifted, except for the fact that we were consistently told that we were. (Male, age 50)

If anything, I feel more inadequate than superior because there are people, I don't know if you want to call them geniuses, who are clearly brilliant theoreticians.... I can't be that.... So I don't feel particularly gifted anymore. (Female, age 42)

I don't consider myself gifted. I consider myself above average in intelligence; somebody who's worked hard to get where she is. (Female, age 41)

I was very confused by the word, gifted.... It's a euphemism, and to some extent was meant to be euphemistic, not to be completely understandable to the children. They were very concerned about us getting swelled heads. I remember saying, 'I don't have a lot of gifts.' (Male, age 50)

I don't think of the term (gifted) as relevant to life. There are smarter people out there than I am. I'm aware of that. But I don't feel superior in any way to anybody else. I'm aware I can see things.... I think of myself as being quicker than other people, not smarter than other people. (Female, age 49)

Milgram (1990) identified specific creative talent as one of four categories of giftedness, asserting that "one way to identify specific creative talent in children before these abilities become fully realized in their vocations is by examining leisure-time, out-of-school activities" (p. 217). Milgram found that although gifted children and adolescents indulge in nonintellectual pursuits, like television viewing and game playing, many devote their leisure time to activities designed to satisfy their curiosity and help to develop their interests. Reading, practicing skills, and perfecting techniques associated with specific interests and talents consume much of the free time of gifted children (Milgram, 1990, p. 222).

Many of the Hunter respondents shared a quality that has been traditionally associated with being gifted: reading as a pastime central to their lives. Terman also found that the gifted children in his studies read more frequently, widely, and at an earlier age than those in an unselected control group. According to Cox (1981), "Perhaps the leisure-time activity most characteristic of gifted children, except for the very young, is reading" (p. 112). Cox found reading to be "the favorite free-time activity identified most often by the gifted subjects...In addition to reading for fun, gifted subjects read selective topics to gather information for special projects in school, to support their interests in a great many hobbies, to explore new interests, and to further their understanding of a sport or some other recreational activity" (pp. 112-113).

Cox further suggested that the reason for the significant amount of reading done by the gifted is "to satisfy their curiosity, which is one of the most pervasive characteristics of their kind" (p. 113). According to Hollingworth (1975, pp. 272-273),

> It appears that the gifted know more games of intellectual skill, such as bridge, and chess; that they care less, age for age, for play which involves predominantly simple sensorimotor activity which is aimless; and that gifted girls are far less interested in traditional girls' play, as with dolls and tea sets, than unselected girls are. The gifted enjoy more complicated and more highly competitive games than the generality do, age for age. Outdoor sports hold a high place with the gifted, being almost as popular among them as is reading.

Hildreth (1952) reported in *Educating Gifted Children at Hunter College Elementary School* that a questionnaire investigating the leisure-time activities of the children revealed that reading was found to be far and above the most popular pursuit. Drawing, painting, sports, skating, and music were listed as pastimes along with dancing, horseback riding, imaginative play, bicycling, and games (p. 182). Hildreth reported "very low percentages for television, movies, and radio", which she found difficult to understand. She suggested that "the considerable percentages for drawing and painting, music, imaginative play, and some others were somewhat surprising as 'favorite activities,' but these preferences no doubt reflect the excellent guidance given in these areas by the 'special' teachers" (p. 183). Some very high-IQ children are unable to find peers of similar intellect and engage in solitary play. These children, among them those who achieve eminence later in life, are known to delve into their interests with great zeal and concentration (Hollingworth, 1975, pp. 273-274). Although the leisure-time activities of the gifted are varied, reading is almost universally engaged in and consumes much of these youngsters' time.

When queried about their special interests during childhood, some respondents mentioned art, foreign language, politics, and music, but few ended up with vocations as creative artists. Many, however, voiced enthusiasm for the special classes offered at Hunter (see Chapter 2, The Teachers section). It appears then that the one leisure-time activity most consistently mentioned during childhood was reading, and that this pastime became a significant part of the lives of the respondents.

I knew that I was reading way beyond what other people were reading when I was pulled out of the regular public school, and I knew that I was complimented a lot for being very independent and smart.... Reading is still my favorite pastime, so much so, that I've managed to live without a TV and not miss it. (Female, age 50)

I often sat in class while other things were going on and I was just reading my book. Sometimes the whole class would get up and leave, and I would still keep reading. (Female, age 48)

I'm never without something to read. It used to be fiction, mostly, but in recent years, it is much more likely to be factual material. At the moment, in my back pocket are four or five magazine articles I've clipped to read when I get a chance. If I haven't read the *Times* yet, and I get to the subway with nothing much to read, I'll buy another copy, even though there is one waiting for me at home. (Male, age 49)

Although there was little uniformity in how subjects defined giftedness, most respondents agreed that they belonged at the school.

I absolutely felt I belonged there.... From the minute I arrived at Hunter, I felt like...I'd come home. (Male, age 44)

My recollection is when I read my literary creations, certainly when I thought about my own reactions to AVE [Audio-Visual Education] and heard others, absolutely [I belonged at Hunter]. When I knew that at best I was a solid check in French, and there were plenty of other "pluses" around me, I would say I was fully aware of the fact that I was in the third 20% at Hunter. And maybe I was smack in the middle. I definitely felt that there were some that were below me, but I certainly knew that there was a horde ahead of me. (Male, age 49)

A few felt they did not belong at Hunter, though not because of their intellectual ability.

Most of the Hunter kids in those days were middle- and upper-middle-class kids living in the Upper East Side and Upper West Side. I and a few others were from the Lower East Side. My parents had very humble occupations and backgrounds compared to the other kids.... The typical Hunter kid had a nice elevator apartment, white-collar parents, a different lifestyle, a car, alternating current. We lived in a walk-up on 15th Street that had direct current. We didn't have electric trains and stuff like that, so it was always a big treat to visit other people's houses. In the days of the Second World War, in case of civil disaster, they had a system of notification with class mothers.... the school would call the class mother in a pyramid system to notify everybody. My mother worked during the day, my father worked during the night, so he was the class mother...I was always embarrassed by that. (Male, age 49)

I was a very fragile kid who cried very easily and was very emotional. My family problems made it hard for me to feel comfortable. My report cards said 'very emotional, etc.' I probably would have been better off, had my parents had the money, at a smaller private school where my emotional problems would have gotten more attention. (Male, age 39)

I never felt I belonged there.... I felt like a misfit, but that was my own personal view of myself and I don't blame the school for that...Since we were intellectually superior, life was [supposed to be] wonderful and there were no problems...there was no understanding that there was a great deal of pain there most probably. (Female, age 43)

Those who felt they were not "Hunter material" in an intellectual sense were a small minority. For example:

If Hunter was for the absolute 99.99 percentile, I guess that meant you were a solid 160 IQer and that maybe I was a solid 135 IQer, and if I were thrust in there and got the guilt associated with not performing, I guess the answer would have to be NO. I think I survived there; I think I did what I had to do and I think I got my share of pluses, but it was harmful because I'm sure that the school, and certainly the school coupled with my mother, the child psychologist, put a lot of stress on me. (Male, age 49)

A majority of the respondents appear to be individuals whose options and actions are governed by their self-image as capable of significant achievement. Whether any of these former students who were educated at what was considered the foremost school for highly gifted children in the United States have used their "gifts" to attain the highest level of accomplishment in their field still remains to be seen. Many of those interviewed regarded their giftedness with mixed emotions. While recognizing their greater capacity to learn and to achieve, the former students were largely restrained, even humble

humble about their abilities and eager to assert that intelligence is measured by much more than a standardized test.

ON BEING DIFFERENT

At Hunter, I was one of many like me, and experienced a warm sense of belonging.... Later, I was thrust into the real world with a bang. I felt different, even freakish, when my interests were alien to those around me. Even my vocabulary had to be stifled.

The beginning of a child's schooling marks a significant step in individuation, the awareness of the self as distinct and apart from others. Children labeled as gifted often feel a heightened sense of difference from those not identified as gifted. The recognition of this divergence from others can manifest itself as a feeling of inferiority or superiority (Janos & Robinson, 1985a; Janos, Fung, & Robinson, 1985), and often lasts into adulthood. Because the respondents of the present study were placed among a high-IQ cohort from their earliest school experience, many did not experience a feeling of separation from children of a wider range of measured mental ability until they were older. As they grew up, however, and entered into groups composed of diverse fellow students, many children from Hunter realized that they were indeed different.

I know I require a great deal of stimulation to keep my mind busy and active. I feel the majority of people with average intelligence can take a great deal of time to do mundane things and they live at a much slower pace than I do. I love to see how things work; I'm curious about everything. (Female, age 43)

I have never felt that I fit in my neighborhood. My values and the things I like to do are different from those of the people around me.... I feel different all the time except when I'm in my university setting, and even then, sometimes. (Female, age 48)

As a result of a 1948 *Life Magazine* article entitled "Genius School," a number of interviewees reported feeling self-conscious about the label. Another individual remembers hearing a teacher speak of "outsiders," reinforcing the belief that there indeed was a difference between the Hunter children and the rest of the world. Many admit that feeling different was, and still is, tantamount to feeling superior. Most, on the other hand, will attempt to temper the effect of this assessment by stating that they recognize its impact on others.

I had tickets for "Ah Wilderness"...but the playbill had both this and another O'Neill play in the same issue. At the theater I'm listening to this conversation. "Oh I wonder what they are doing. They must have put these two plays together," and I couldn't stand it, and I turned around and said: "No, they are playing them in repertory," and they were very nice about it, and they thanked me. And I was thinking all these nasty things about suburban ladies who didn't know anything and why were they here anyway, when they belonged at 'Cats.' And one of them said after intermission, and we were waiting for the curtain, "I really should go to the library and get out the book!" I thought, how wonderful! I really liked that. That's the kind of intellectual snobbery that's in me. And I think that is how I see myself as being different. And I find myself, every once in a while, getting irritated with people. I pick something up, one, two, three, and that's a very bad characteristic. It's not fair. I find myself doing it...I fight it, but I find myself getting very annoyed if things aren't done the right way and quickly. (Female, age 48)

I feel different from others, smarter, snobbishly smarter. It's very hard. I get very impatient with people who don't pick up things quickly, actually. People who work for me probably find it nice in some ways and also very maddening. And I know it drives my children crazy. (Female, age 47)

I very often feel a step ahead of what somebody is saying. Sometimes I'm wrong, but a lot of times, I have already arrived there. If there's a joke, I find myself laughing at it before it has been said, and I'm the only one laughing. You can't tell people you feel different. They think you're snobbish or whatever, but it isn't that. You might value people for whatever reason, but you really are different in some respects. (Female, age 48)

I was in the film business for twenty years and writing magazine articles for a lot of that time, and I got to the point where it just got to be methodical because I knew how to do it. I knew all the questions and I knew all the answers. I had to change professions, and business suddenly is a great new game for me to learn and to play. (Male, age 38)

One respondent found her "differences" less of an intellectual issue and more of a socioeconomic one:

I lived on the Lower East Side, although I came from a professional family. My father was a doctor, my mother was a nurse and later a social worker, and a school teacher. We were misfits.... And I had this long schlepp up to Hunter and most of the kids lived on the Upper East Side or the Upper West Side, and most of their parents didn't want them to visit me because I lived in the 'slums.' And I felt socially at a disadvantage. I was always going to be mixing with my betters, and sort of trying to pass as their socioeconomic equal. I was usually their intellectual equal but their socioeconomic equal, I never have been. (Female, age 48)

Later this psychologist stated:

> I can enjoy a variety of people: I have had experience in a work situation where I think I have been resented for my abilities, and that can be extremely uncomfortable. But in say, personal life or socializing, I don't feel that I have only to socialize with big brains. One of the things I sort of pride myself on is that I can talk to anybody about anything. I can talk to a lady on a bus about recipes, because I am interested in recipes.... I feel different from the general population, but I don't think that this recognition was always there. For example, when I was, I think, a senior in college, I began to delineate who was really my group.... And I guess my feeling of being different from the general population is an ever-increasing one, and it isn't just a matter of intelligence. I mean in the '80s it's been very much a matter of values.... So that intelligence alone isn't the criterion by which you seek your comrades.

Other respondents described feeling isolated because of their intelligence.

> On the negative side, you're a little bit more isolated when you know you're special in some way.

> When I was taking an intensive course in Danish in Denmark, I learned to take my [test] papers back upside down so that other people couldn't see that there were hardly any red marks on them. There are very few people I can talk to about this kind of thing, and that's why I cherish my Hunter friends. (Female, age 48)

> On the negative side, perhaps one could say you're a little bit more isolated when you know that you are 'special' in some way. It was a personal, private isolation that even exists today.... There's also a sense of isolation inside of yourself; will people really understand where I'm headed; will my spouse, my partner, my new friend accept this for what it is? (Female, age 38)

Judging from the responses to the question, "As a high-IQ child now grown up, do you think your IQ itself has led to a life qualitatively different from the lives of people of average IQ?" many interviewees agreed that their intellect had ordered their lives in a manner that is discernably different from most others.

> I tend to judge people—an important aspect of my liking them or getting along with them—if they're intelligent enough. It [high IQ] does make you see things and live life differently. (Female, age 46)

> I've always identified IQ not so much with being smart but with intellectual curiosity. Life for me is a perpetual school. I will find a

subject the same way that you will find a subject when you're in school and read about it for two years until I know all I can know about it, or until I get bored. I don't know that the average person bothers to do that.... They don't want to know everything...they just want to be entertained. I've always wondered what high IQ really means. It's not just how fast you can put the blocks together...it's the state of the mind...of having a sense of your own identity and wanting to develop yourself to the point where you are happy just because you're learning.... A love of fun combined with a high IQ has led to my being ecstatically happy in the pursuit of knowledge. (Male, age 38)

I think there is enormous impact. On the plus side, I think I'm able to get more out of life sometimes because I'm more thoughtful, or perhaps I attempt to learn about something I'm not familiar with as I go along. I also can hold my own a little bit better in a conversation or in a meeting.... You kind of watch out not to floor people too soon or let them figure you out, because this country is democratic in more ways than one, and we often don't like the person who sticks out in one way or another. (Female, age 38)

Perhaps high-IQ people have a sense of more possibilities and less often feel like victims. We have more ways of taking charge of our lives or more different options. I don't know how to do a lot of things, but do have the sense that to a large extent, I can control my life. People aren't controlling it for me. (Female, age 39)

The influences that have caused me to be idealistic in combination with the fact that I felt I was bright made me believe that I had the capacity to do some things that other people might not be able to do. I have the motivation that came from my family and background, and the intellect as well, to be able to effect certain kinds of changes and do some things that others might not be able to do. Yes, IQ does contribute. (Male, age 38)

You have a lot of things that you have to come to terms with. You're talking to someone and you have gotten the gist, they told you something in one sentence, and you have seen exactly where they are headed, and you want to say, "Okay, let's get on with it!" and you can't. You have to allow people to say what they want to say. They don't believe that you understand what they are going to say, and you do.... Nobody likes a know-it-all. Most often I have found...that I am right most of the time. And I really do trust my own instincts, only I don't believe that they are just instincts anymore. It's the ability to see what is going on, to get it all together, to synthesize it, and to know the consequences. And that's hard to live with, because...people don't want to hear it, and the consequences aren't always so great, so some people think you are like a Cassandra.

You want to get in there and intervene and change things, and nobody wants you doing that all the time. It's difficult. I have to sit back. I have learned, particularly as a supervisor, because most of the time I could say to one of the people who works for me, 'If you do that, that is going to happen, and you don't want that to happen.' The fact is, I have got to let them do it. Even if I know that they are going to fail. First of all, I can't let them know that they are going to fail because then who is going to try anymore? And I can't say, 'I told you so!' at the end. I just have to support them, and have learned to be able to do that, but it was a long time coming. (Female, age 37)

My tendency toward life is to always gravitate toward people who are unusual or remarkable, even more so than myself. I'm very attracted to very gifted people, and I like to engage them and be stimulated by them. (Female, age 49)

A small number of respondents indicated that they might have been better off if their IQs had not been quite so high.

I'm generally inclined to think that I would have been a much happier person if I hadn't been as intelligent as I was. That if I had just been bright enough, I would have had a more normal and happier life.... I have three degrees, including a law degree, and yet I haven't really experienced a great deal of satisfaction...or success.... I think it's a problem of being overqualified. (Male, age 40)

I don't know if it's the high IQ that's done it, but sometimes I say to myself there would be advantages to being a pig satisfied rather than Socrates unsatisfied. (Male, age 44)

Although most agree that their high IQs have made their lives qualitatively different from those of average intellect, a number of those surveyed felt that the effect has been minor.

It's better than being subnormal, that's for sure, but I think we're pretty much like a lot of other people. (Female, age 49)

I really don't think my IQ has had much effect on the quality of my life, but maybe that's because I'm sort of on the lazy side.... I was just never in the habit of exerting myself, and to this day, I have an attention deficit disorder. I don't think that I'm a better or worse pediatrician than any other, except that I remember more. And no one will play Trivial Pursuit [board game] with me.... I was on Jeopardy [TV game show] last year...I won $31,000 in two nights. So the only different thing in my life is that I've been on Jeopardy, and most people I know haven't. (Male, age 43)

In general, I don't feel different from other people, but I am aware that I do catch things faster than others. I can perceive patterns more rapidly, patterns of behavior, political patterns, socioeconomic patterns; but I don't view myself as being smarter. To me, it's faster. Smarter is somebody who has a better retention of names and dates than I do—trivia. (Female, age 47)

I think that a high IQ just isn't enough. I'm fortunate enough to have figured out, somewhere along the way, that brains are not enough, and that there are many other qualities that you have to combine with that in order to succeed. By succeed, I mean accomplish what you want to accomplish, whatever that might be at the time. It takes more than just intelligence. (Female, age 39)

I always went under the assumption that I'm smart, and I think that can't help but have an effect on your life.... So having that confidence is really nice. But the other part is, I think it's my personality that has helped me to get a lot further than necessarily high IQ. In the end, I think personality is definitely as important. (Female, age 39)

I think it has had an impact, but I don't only think that it's my IQ that mattered. I'm well-rounded, and I get along, and my personality was substantially enhanced by my IQ, and rather than being a well-varied person with an 80 IQ, it's better if you're a well-varied person with a 119 IQ. But I think hard work, or pursuing things, had more effect. (Male, age 41)

Most of the individuals interviewed were quick to pinpoint the considerable positive aspects of their giftedness.

I think the fact that I'm smarter has given me more of a handle on what goes on in life and has helped negate some of the actual emotional problems I've had by simply giving me something to think about other than myself. (Female, age 49)

It seems self-evident to me that my life is preoccupied with intellectual matters. Writing and computers are both activities that require greater intelligence than average. People who do well in them generally are smarter people. There's no question that matters of the intellect are important to me. (Male, age 38)

It has made it possible to do things that I could not have done without it. I've been able to understand things; I've been able to make a success financially, and that comes from the ability to think just a little bit faster and a little bit better. It's not dramatically better; it comes easily. That may be a drawback. It has tended to make me a little lazier than probably would have been a good idea. On the other hand, I was able to succeed. (Male, age 49)

It's been a great benefit. I pretty easily freelanced in a difficult field in music and made a living at it for a long time. When I decided that I was pretty bored at it, and wanted to get into another field, it wasn't that difficult to get involved in a very big growth field like computer software and find a niche in it. It has been a plus. It gives you more resources. (Male, age 39)

I've gone an academic and intellectual route, so I've gone in a direction that gives me pleasure and that I'm good at. I'm not artistic, I'm not athletic, so I didn't go in other directions.... The route that I've taken has given me pleasure...(Female, age 46)

I think most people seek fulfillment through material life and possessions and external signs of success, and judging by society's standards, none of us can get away from that conditioning...My values, I think, are very different; I would certainly say that high IQ, which is just not intelligence, but I would say 'concernment,' sensitivity, and perception of things that are subtle, made my likes and dislikes more subtle.... My values tend to be spiritual values, and the creative, the aesthetic, and the spiritual are basically my modus operandi with regard to my life. (Female, age 42)

High IQ is a pretty valuable entity. It takes other personality qualities too, but I don't think I would have gone on to be as successful if I weren't smart. (Female, age 47)

Weighing the question of feeling different from others, the respondents admitted some pride and gratification with what they perceived as their heightened capacities, and a keen recognition of how these gifts have enhanced their quality of life. Although these differences were viewed largely as positive factors, a number admitted some negative attitudes in areas of socialization, namely feeling isolated from most others and exhibiting behaviors that cause others discomfort. Yet, whatever personal or professional path they traveled, virtually all the respondents, if given the choice, would not have relinquished their special skills and talents.

chapter 4
The Family

School is not the only significant factor affecting the development of high-IQ children. Parental attitudes and family environment are at least as important (Albert, 1978; Marjoribanks, 1979). None of our Hunter subjects spent his or her whole day at school; in fact, at 2:00 p.m. the school day was over.

The staff at Hunter expected cooperation from the parents of the students in furthering and fostering the goals and values presented at the school. Apparently, the Hunter faculty did not feel they always received adequate cooperation.

> The traditional failings of the gifted child that are due largely to unwise management can be counteracted by taking certain precautions in home training. The Hunter faculty are always ready to guide parents in the home training of the gifted when they are invited to do so. There are always some who resent unsolicited advice from "old maids." (Hildreth, 1952, p. 177)

Any teacher might hope for support and reinforcement at home, but Hunter seemed to expect more than that.

> Parents have been advised to take their children off the professional radio and television programs when these public exhibitions seemed to be turning them into smart alecks. (Hildreth, 1952, p. 177)

Parents were encouraged to try to enrich their child's experience at home, and to give responsibility when possible, but were also advised:

> Do not exaggerate the child's superiority or make him unduly conscious

of it....Avoid commenting on the child's brilliance in his presence. (Hildreth, 1952, p. 177)

This chapter will examine the influences of the family and the attitudes of parents and other family members toward their gifted children.

PREVIOUS RESEARCH

Many researchers have suggested that the family plays a significant role in a gifted child's performance, both in school and later on. Albert (1980a) stated

> Most explanations for the differences between promise and fulfillment point to substantial differences in early facilitating environments, family factors, and educational-career opportunities. (p. 174)

In an earlier review of studies of early development of high achievers, Albert (1978) found

> The consensus of these studies is that the creative person-to-be comes from a family that is anything but harmonious—one which has built into its relationships, its organization of roles, and its levels of communication a good deal of tension if not disturbance at times, what I term a "wobble." But along with these characteristics, there is a commitment to achievement as opposed to just "having fun," a special focus of interest and aspirations upon the indexed child, and a great deal of family effort to see that these aspirations are met. (pp. 203-204)

Ochse (1990) commented further

> There is much evidence to support these suggestions and further to indicate that the childhood homes of creative achievers, both past and present, were typically rich in opportunity and encouragement to achieve intellectually, but poor in emotional comforts. From the evidence, one may indeed go so far as to suggest that creators typically suffered some deprivation and distress in childhood. (p. 81)

Given what we now know about families, it is doubtful that emotional distress is unique to or even distinctive of families of high achievers, but valuing intellectual achievement does appear to be especially prevalent in these families.

Colangelo and Dettmann (1983) called attention to "the importance of home environment and family relations on the later achievement of high-ability youngsters" (p. 25), but pointed out that "there is still considerable confusion in terms of what the major family influences are" (p. 25). Similarly, Janos and Robinson (1985b) stated that "familial influences on the development of intellectual giftedness are poorly described despite their central role" (p. 182).

Albert (1980a) offered some clues to the way the family might function.

> Families are defined as experience-producing (generating) and experience-selecting (directing) agents in the development of their members, especially the younger ones. Furthermore, parental experiences, behaviors, and personalities give form and substance to these two basic family functions. (p. 174)

Earlier studies of gifted individuals have identified certain family psychodynamics as relevant. Roe (1953) noted in her study of 64 eminent male scientists that they were typically the eldest children in middle-class families and sons of professional men. Most had experienced either illness or a severe disruption in family life—death of a parent or divorce—at an early age.

Goertzel and Goertzel (1962) found "a passive father and a dominant mother who promoted the child's welfare above all else." Again, some major negative experience seems also to be a factor. Van Tassel-Baska (1989) speculated that adversity appears to teach certain lessons about perseverance and achievement.

Investigating the backgrounds of successful blacks, Clark (1983) found parental attitudes and expectations to be extremely important. Other studies (Brandwein, 1955; Witty, 1930) emphasized the significance of home environment and parental influences. Bloom and Sosniak (1981) also mentioned that in many cases a parent has a specific talent, skill, or ability which the child is encouraged to explore in depth. The parent provides a model, as well as encouragement and support, and

> Small signs of interest and capability in the talent field by any of these children were encouraged and much rewarded by the parents. (p. 88)

THE HUNTER SAMPLE

Parental attitudes and influences were volunteered by half of our interviewees. Clearly, parental attitudes are significant to some extent for all Hunter students because parents make the initial decision to apply for admission. Some subjects mentioned parental concern about elitism as something that made the parents hesitate to send their children to a school like Hunter.

> I really should have gone to Hunter earlier. The teachers in my school wanted me to. My parents were reluctant to let me go, but finally under a lot of pressure from my elementary school, which was not a very good elementary school, they buckled under. (Male, age 44)

Some parents, having made the decision to send the child to a special school, tried to ameliorate the influence by playing down the specialness of the experience.

> It wasn't made a big deal of. For example, it was my parent's wisdom and restraint. They weren't saying "Oh, you know, he goes to the Hunter school" to a friend so that I would sort of pick up that there was something there. (Male, age 45)

> I remember asking my mother what my IQ was and having her refuse to tell me....I think she refused so I wouldn't get swell-headed. (Male, age 42)

> When the article came out in *Life Magazine* with the headline "The Genius School," I remember my father having an argument with my brother and telling him that he couldn't argue with me because I was a genius. I'm sure he was being sarcastic, because he explained to me classes like that had a range and I shouldn't jump to conclusions. (Female, age 48)

Parents often seemed to have taken a certain pride in having a gifted child at Hunter.

> At Hunter, I was encouraged to do whatever I could to be the best. My home environment also encouraged that. (Female, age 48)

> My parents made me feel smart and talented before I went to Hunter. (Female, age 44)

> My family contributed to it a great deal too, especially my mother, because she encouraged that atmosphere of specialness, and "Oh, isn't it wonderful that you can read and recite from the Constitution," and when you're eighteen months old you just turn into a showoff, but you don't know it. (Female, age 49)

> I knew I was brighter, I knew I was special. My parents were always telling me that. I didn't know that it was a special class or a special school because it was the only school I ever went to and my brother also went there. (Male, age 41)

Some individuals, though, reported a very different kind of experience. Instead of parental pride and support, they experienced competition or pressure.

> I had a very unhappy home situation where my parents were actually very intimidated by my being a gifted child. And they were determined that I be normal. In fact, I had gotten scholarships to private school after Hunter, and they wouldn't send me to private school. So I rebelled by almost flunking out of high school....I've often felt that my two years at Hunter practically saved my life. They were really a basis of something positive that I was able to get back to in college....I grew up in a house, and probably no one else will say this to you, where there was not a single book, a single picture on the wall, no record player, no FM radio, no magazine subscriptions, and the only thing going on was the television. And Hunter was for me like being the kid in the candy store, except better. So it really absolutely changed my life. (Male, age 44)

> I always felt that I was above average, that's all. And being a product in those years of a mother who was a child psychologist, I always considered that I had an uphill battle because I always thought that more was expected of me than I could deliver. (Male, 49)

> When I was in Hunter, I was very eager to do whatever kinds of assignments I was given. In fact, I remember laboring over them considerably, and I remember wanting to have my papers perfect. And if I made a mistake, I would write them over. And my mother was very angry at this, that I would spend so much time on my work at Hunter. (Female, age 49)

Some parents learned that it was possible to apply too much pressure.

> My sister had also gone to Hunter Elementary, and was later pushed into the two-year acceleration program at Bronx Science. And she was really a nervous wreck and had a lot of physical problems her senior year...that were caused by the stress of trying to do well in a short period of time. My mother saw what happened to my sister and saw what was happening to me, and decided that she would dig up some money and put me in a private school. It was a good idea. (Male, age 39)

Parental attitudes may not have been so obvious to elementary school subjects at the time, but later those attitudes became clearer, and seemed to affect the choices our subjects made around issues of success and achievement. Consider the following responses:

> I wish that I had taken some time off before going to college. My parents wouldn't have subsidized me for a year the way I subsidize my children. They couldn't afford it, and it wasn't in their parenting style to allow their children to make decisions....I guess my whole life has been

arranged to avoid hassles, because my parents hassled me so much. So I live a life that is relatively hassle-free. (Male, age 43)

A psychiatrist may be able to answer better than I, but I think I was held back by the training within my family, which was that there was somehow a message to me that ambition was not to be prized. Maybe it was the reaction of a child trying not to outdo his parents....I'm not sure, but part of me was always pulled back. I can't imagine that Hunter had any effect on holding me down. I think on some level Hunter exposed me to possibilities, and to the disappointment of not seeing those possibilities fulfilled in the people who were immediately around me. I saw a lot of people at Hunter who came from families where there was a greater sense of success, of people having used opportunities well and having done things with their lives. And I always felt that Hunter regrettably made me more conscious of the limitations I felt about my father's use of his own talents. (Male, age 48)

I wish that I had gotten away from my mother. If I had, I think that I would be a lot better off. Now, I don't know what that means, but I do know that my mother is an emotional swamp. I went to City College and continued to live at home, and what I should have done was go to Alaska or Hawaii or California and make my life myself. In which case I would have been able to think about what I wanted to do, and not have been in this horrible parasitic, or whatever it was, relationship with her. (Female, age 49)

Parents have expectations for their children, and their expectations can lead to a variety of pressures, but the most common seems to be the expectation that the children will follow the same career choice as the parent. Three male subjects observed:

My father was an international lawyer, and he definitely wanted me and my brother to become lawyers, but neither of us was interested, and he never pushed us. He was a deeply involved socialist, and I think the greatest disappointment of his life was that neither of his sons became politically interested in the least. (Male, age 38)

My father was a physician and psychiatrist, and I had early on sort of thought about [doing] that, and although there was a transient competition among some other [professions], that pretty much was what really interested me, and the rest of my life sort of confirmed these original perceptions. (Male, age 45)

My father was only a sixth-grade student, but a self-educated man, and a true intellectual for knowledge's sake. I never was that type of person. It was one of the problems I had later on, that my father was an intellectual and he never went to school, and I wanted to be like that. And I knew that I had a deep dark secret that he couldn't find out—that I wasn't! Male, age 41)

Siblings played a lesser role than parents in shaping experiences during the Hunter years. It was not unusual for younger brothers and sisters to follow at Hunter, and the school policy was generally to enroll them if they met the admissions criteria. This sometimes led to a different kind of pressure.

> I think I had a tremendous sibling rivalry with my brother....Even as an adult my mother would say, "But it's the truth, you just were never as bright as your brother."...I always saw myself as the young child. (Female, age 40)

On the other hand, for children without siblings, Hunter could provide a sense of relief from the isolation of being an only child.

> From the age of three on, I had the company of all these extraordinary children, who just landed on my doorstep. That was an amazing advantage, that compensated for the lack of siblings. It was terrific company. (Female, age 46)

Generally, the quotations above suggest that the family influenced tremendously the attitudes of our subjects toward their own intelligence and toward the issues of career, success, and achievement. Consider the following:

> I think it's more the values that I have and the traditions that have been passed down by my family that have contributed to my success. (Female, age 43)

> I think that the home ambiance was probably as significant or more significant than anything that happened at school. (Male, age 42)

> How much imput does the immediate family have in your formative years? I mean your IQ is one thing, but if you are a brilliant child growing up in a sterile environment you are not going to reach your potential. I think that my family was very influential. Not just my parents, but my grandfather too. (Female, age 45)

The mood in the home is an important factor in any child's performance in school and later in life. Typically, children adopt a position of either compliance or defiance toward parental expectations. Compliance is more common in childhood, defiance in adolescence.

As we noted earlier, most of the Hunter students during the years of our study came from middle-class homes. Their parents were usually professionals, with a respect for learning and education, and a set of expectations that included academic and professional achievement. These parents wanted their children to do well, to bring pride to the family.

On the other hand, some respondents cited parental ambivalence as being a factor that might have made it harder for them to reach their fullest potential and surpass their parents in social, academic, or professional accomplishment. It is clear from the interviews that at least several of our subjects understood the parental message "Do well, but not too well."

chapter 5
Competition and Rivalry

When the faculty and administration designed the program at Hunter College Elementary School, they decided to actively minimize competition between the students. They believed that motivating students toward individual success at the expense of the needs of others was not in the best interests of society. An attempt was made to balance academic challenge with social and interpersonal skills. Hildreth (1952), in her book *Educating Gifted Children at Hunter College Elementary School,* describes the school's goal in this way:

> The Hunter school staff believes that gifted children should be educated so as to achieve the richest possible life for themselves and at the same time help to achieve the most rewarding life for their fellow members of society (p. 42)....Instead of selfish striving to show off one's superior accomplishments or to get ahead of someone else, to attain the highest prize or the first place, they learn to work for the good of the whole enterprise. (p. 73)

Respondents to our questionnaire and personal interviews expressed some of their strongest opinions and feelings about this issue. They discussed the effects of competition in two main areas: with regard to their classmates at Hunter, and afterward at other schools and in adulthood.

COMPETITION AT HUNTER

An unexpected result of our survey of graduates was that although many people had strong feelings about the issue of competition, these feelings reflected completely opposite experiences. Approximately half the respondents thought that Hunter was extremely competitive, considering it a negative aspect of their education there, with serious detrimental after-effects. Only one person who perceived the environment as competitive found it to be in any way positive. An almost equal number of interviewees remembered very little or no competition, or recall it being actively discouraged. This group is more evenly divided between those for whom the policy of discouraging interpersonal competition was positive, and those for whom it created some problems and difficulties, particularly later on in high school and college.

The source for this paradoxical outcome probably lies in the HCES tradition of granting instructional and curricular independence to its teachers (see Chapter 8).

Because it was the intention of the Hunter administration to minimize or even eliminate competition, we will examine first the comments of those students who thought this goal was successfully accomplished.

I value most about my experience at Hunter the community of bright children....That was an excellent situation for me to grow up in. I really appreciated the company. I was not aware in any way that I was in a competitive situation. I have no memory that it was. (Female, age 46)

I think everybody at Hunter was aware that we were gifted, and I remember seeing a piece of paper that had everybody's IQ scores on it. But I don't think that made us any better than anybody else. I never felt competitive in that school, not at all. (Female, age 43)

I never felt that I was in an extremely competitive environment which would make me feel less than somebody else. I don't know if that was because that doesn't happen much in the younger grades or whether the school was just very well run. I did go to competitive schools later on. There I felt the competitiveness much more....[At Hunter] I was with people who accepted me for what I was, and people who were like me....It was a was comfortable environment, very relaxed. It was not an anxious place, as I found in other schools. (Male, age 38)

I just didn't feel competitive there. I didn't see much competition. (Female, age 44)

Compared to how much kids grade-grub today and compare and so on, this was rather a blissful time. We didn't have grades and we didn't have "I got and you got" that I remember at all. So I think that a lot of the atomosphere was the sense that the people who were there did belong there and the let's get on with our business. (Female, age 48)

A number of respondents felt that, although it might have been pleasant at the time, the lack of competitiveness they experienced created problems for them later on.

Hunter was very non-competitive....[My experiences there] were comfortable, they were friendly, they were warm. I wasn't prepared to be thrown into a non-nurturing environment. I don't know if that's Hunter's fault. but certainly it was noncompetitive. Even the grades: check, check plus. Nobody ever got a minus. You either got a check or a check-plus....(Female, age 47)

There was no level of competition there that I remember. Actually, sometimes that germ of competition is what's needed to make someone rise to the top of the pack. We were comfortably working to our utmost but nobody would kill themselves to prove that they were brighter than the next guy....I guess in a heterogeneous situation you want to make sure that everyone knows you can do better and you scramble. We didn't scramble. When we wanted to do something it was there for us to do....You never had to fight for it. Maybe it's that lack of motivation that later on in life keeps people from accomplishing more. (Female, age 44)

I think it failed to prepare me because at Hunter there was no emphasis on grades or on competition or on structured learning. So that when I went on to junior high school it was a great shock, and I had to get adjusted to a much more traditional, more organized type of education, and I probably never learned to put as much stress on grades as other students did because they had a much more traditional type of elementary school experience. (Male, age 40)

There was a lot of freedom in how far you wanted to go, and if you wanted to go far, nobody was ever going to stop you. If you were going to be lazy, I don't remember anybody setting any fires under me. And I felt weak in math, which I don't have any inherent gift for. I always got the feeling that maybe I skipped something....There were things like that I felt I had to get later....I think they let me have my own way a little too much. (Female, age 49)

It very poorly prepared me for Hunter High School, which is ironic and puzzling. The high school was very competitive, brought in a lot of kids from outside the early Hunter environment. A lot of homework, a lot of self-discipline and self-motivation required of us. In elementary school, right up through sixth grade, there was very, very little homework. It was more an emphasis on developing the intellect. I think they were a little too hung up on the "intellectually gifted" concept, as though if you made it through your biennial IQ test then don't worry about it. I felt very poorly prepared. I think most of the kids who went through the elementary school had a tough adjustment once they got to the high school. (Female, age 39)

I was unprepared to work in school. It had always been sort of playtime. When I got into public junior high school, they descended on me with a lot of stuff, which I just wasn't used to. (Male, age 49)

My kids went to a competitive school, they did not go to a nurturing school. That was my choice. I guess I've given them something I've lacked. Will they be better for it? Time will tell. A lot of people said "Oh, they're at that school. It's so competitive there. How can you do it?" My sense is that my kids were never aware of being in a competitive situation. They learned that some people go to worse schools and some people are A+ and if they want to be A+ they have to put out a little more. (Female, age 45)

One respondent gave a specific example of how the attempt to eradicate competition created a negative experience for him.

It's hard for me to intuit what the Hunter policy was toward competition, but it probably didn't work. We were the most tested children around. Even though test scores were supposedly hidden from us we learned how to find the results. On report cards, we didn't receive numerical or letter grades, but a plus for improving, a check for remaining the same, and a minus for slipping, based on our results on standardized tests. I considered myself a math whiz and expected a plus in the subject. My scores kept increasing until I hit the maximum score on the test. The next time I also got the maximum score on the test and my report card only gave me a check for math—no improvement. I knew what had happened and launched a complaint. (Male, age 44)

As mentioned earlier, an equal number of respondents thought that Hunter had failed to eliminate competition among the students. In fact, a number of interviewees seemed to believe that Hunter faculty were actively encouraging competition, and for most of these students, it was a very negative aspect of their experience at Hunter.

I think that the stiff competition and the constant striving to be better turned what could have been a very positive experience into something with very, very negative side effects. I wish children could take the good out of it, which there was a lot of, but remove the competitive environment....I think that the competitiveness and the environment that was set up there was a real hindrance to me later, in that, for example, now I won't even play a game of tennis. I just like to hit the ball. I really kind of burned out, I think because of all the competition I felt in grade school. (Female, age 43)

The biggest underlying theme, the biggest issue of education at Hunter, was competition....I didn't know until I went to college that you didn't go after people when they got their papers back and say "What did you get?"

That was standard technique at Hunter....I think [competition] was generated by everybody. I think even, probably unconsciously, by the teachers. Which was too bad, but we all knew who was first and second, and who was room monitor, and who made noise and who didn't....The children fostered it, and the parents fostered the competition between us, too. I think that's one of the major problems, and I think that it's all-pervasive....The competition issue has its positive and negative sides. I am much more aware of the negative than the positive side. (Female, age 45)

One of the largest negative aspects, I think, is the level of competition that was introduced at all levels of the curriculum. We were being told that we individually had to do well, which meant in effect that we were being compared constantly to each other as individuals. I think we failed to learn to work as a group, failed to really see group projects or group efforts rewarded, and in my later life I certainly felt that to be a strong disadvantage in the way the real world operates. (Female, age 38)

Some remembered very specific details of the way things were structured to encourage a feeling of competitiveness.

We were broken up in school into levels according to A, B, C, and D, and everybody did work at whatever level they were working on. And being in group D a lot of areas, I felt badly about myself, or it helped to enhance the thought that I already felt badly about myself, but I just wasn't competing at a high level and saw myself as not as good as other people. I think for a long time I felt that if I were not in a school that was so advanced I would have done better and outshone people who were working on a lower level. And for a long time after that in my life, I found myself gravitating toward small groups where I could outshine people and compete, and, I guess, picking people in my life who I could prove my excellence and shine being around them. (Female, age 43)

I don't know if the staff were really aware of it, but they created an attitude, a feeling you were special because you were tested and you were told you were gifted. It was just by things said and unsaid...and it was very unpleasant because you were encouraged to show off at Hunter, to show what you could do, to achieve, to be noticed, and in real life that's not a very good way to make friends and be happy. (Female, age 49)

I had a lot of difficulty with Hunter. A lot of it was due to my personal problems, but school was a very pressured environment. It was a model school in that, if you were very bright, you could do well there. It was not a good emotional atmosphere for kids. A lot of kids felt the pressure....Teachers and principals made us aware of different ways that you're supposed to be perfect, you're not supposed to have problems, you're supposed to do well because you are very special, and because everybody wants to get into this school. You happened to be accepted, you had to take a test to get in, and you'd better earn it. (Male, age 39)

Some noted exams and the repeated testing of IQ as contributing to the pressure.

I think Hunter taught me to dislike competition. There was a lot of pressure at Hunter. We were tested all the time. I completely turned away from that in my later years. I was able to do well in high school and I went to [college] but I didn't do well there because I just didn't care.... I really don't like to put myself in a competitive situation. I refer that back to elementary school.... The whole competitive aspect is negative. (Female, age 46)

Only one respondent who experienced the competitive pressures at Hunter saw it as a positive aspect of the experience, especially in regard to later schooling. She said:

In other schooling, including [a special high school], less was expected of the students than was expected at Hunter and we didn't get as much respect. When we were at Hunter we were treated as being mature for our age and a lot was expected and a lot was received. Except for academic grades [in high school], we were not treated as, well, as responsible children. (Female, age 40)

COMPETITION AFTER HUNTER

Even those who didn't experience competitiveness as a student felt pressures and expectations to be someone who would achieve something great. Being separated from "ordinary" children created, for some, an elitist feeling that has interfered with their ability to work with others.

All along I have felt, even in high school, that there was entirely too much hype about the intellectually gifted child. There was entirely too much parental pressure. I never felt it from my parents, but the other kids had very high-pressure parents and you would always hear them talking about the results of their kid's IQ test. The parents were constantly comparing the IQs of their children. Inevitably, that kind of pressure got passed on to the children. The kids were, to varying degrees, aware that they were in a special program, but not everyone really understood what that meant. It had nothing but a negative effect on everyone. It was a very detrimental thing. The school made too much of it. You know how the school was written up in newspapers and magazines and people came and took photographs of us. It was absurd....Instead of taking a perhaps truly innate intelligence and helping to maximize the potential that the child could achieve with that by training with discipline and motivation and hard work and values like that, the school had the attitude that "you don't need that stuff because you're intellectually gifted. Let's do interesting things." That's not what a kid needs to go through life. It's nice to be smart, but it doesn't go very far. If you don't have self-discipline and motivation, and you don't know how to work, and you don't know how to study, and you don't know how to organize your time, it doesn't go very far. (Female, age 39)

I know it drives my husband crazy at times, but [Hunter] absolutely instilled in you a praise for getting it fast, whatever it was, and a disdain for people who didn't get it so fast....That "gifted child" business was horrendous. People were constantly being taken through the classrooms and the words "high-IQ" and "gifted" and that kind of thing was said in our presence. I think that was a big mistake because we got exalted opinions [of ourselves] and some of us were very bright and some of us were not very gifted especially, and it gave you a peculiarly exalted sense of who you were and what you were all about, and I think in some ways colored relationships forever after with people who might not be smart but might be terrific people. That was a very major negative. I think they could have done better if they had masked that from young children better. (Female, age 47)

Obviously it's a great thing to be smart. But it isn't always the only thing. What I've learned is that getting through personal and professional situations often depends on personality, on will, on sensitivity, etc., more than it does on simply having these great ideas or being able to verbalize them. I think that's something that any school for the gifted needs to keep a very clear eye on, just as a school for the intellectually slow child does. You have to teach them life skills in order to survive in a faster-paced society. I think schools for the intellectually gifted need to keep an eye on the fact that you're in society. You don't operate alone—smart, genius, whatever you may be—you're always going to operate with other people around you. (Female, age 38)

Other respondents mentioned various other effects of the Hunter experience on their own competitiveness and striving for achievement. As noted in Chapter 3, all have grappled with the difference between themselves and others, and the implications of that difference.

I think that I didn't like the high expectations. I didn't like and still don't like the term "gifted," and I fail to see how that sets one apart. Because it's not one's intellectual capacity, it's what one does with it. From a very early age, I didn't like being called gifted. (Female, age 43)

I feel less ambitious than other people of my generation. I don't know if that's because I've been able to satisfy myself internally and haven't needed a lot of external gratification. Reading, thinking, talking, etc., have served as their own reward so much that the material rewards didn't seem quite so important. (Male, age 42)

I have a group of friends at the beach who are nice women. Most of them are college-educated; there are some who are not. But it's very obvious that even though I don't try to make my intellectual differences felt, and in a sense I even try to use words with fewer syllables, I try to bring my conversation down to what I think is their level, it's very obvious to them that I am smarter than they are. They persist in calling me "the brain." I try very hard, in a sense, to live this down because I want to be their friend.... And I don't want to be a snob, so I really try not to show off in any way, but there's obviously a difference. (Female, age 49)

There's no equality or inequality about it. There's just the differentness and I'm just called to be me like other people are called to be them. This intelligence is not a superiority, it's just something that happens to be part of me, as other people have something that is a part of them that is just as valuable. (Female, age 43)

I think one thing that I regret is not having tried harder to enter and compete in the college environment. I very deliberately steered away from the special category and went to a school that did not rank among the top schools. What I think I've lost in that is not really occupational, but personal. And yet I very clearly made that decision because I was tired of being singled out as intellectually gifted. I would change that at this stage. (Female, age 38)

OVERVIEW

These recollections from our interviewees suggest that a confusing set of messages was being given to the Hunter children, which could be summarized as "Be outstanding, but don't stand out." In their efforts to create well-rounded, balanced individuals, Hunter taught these children not to compete. In spite of the intention to minimize or even eliminate competition, many of our respondents found the environment to be extremely competitive in a way that actually interfered with their performance and satisfaction. Even had Hunter been successful in eradicating competition, given the realities of the adult world, it is hard to imagine how anyone would accomplish the kind of achievements Hunter was expecting from its graduates without a willingness to compete.

Hildreth (1952) stated quite clearly and emphatically that Hunter's goals were twofold: educational and intellectual opportunity, development, and achievement; and social and interpersonal harmony and facility. Because competition can lead to social discord and disruption, it was to be actively discouraged. Apparently, the designers of Hunter's program saw no conflict between these goals, yet we have to question their results, if not their intentions. If we look at our Hunter graduates, we see doctors, lawyers, teachers. All are competent and socially useful, but there are no superstars. Clearly the world needs doctors, lawyers, and teachers, and the more competent they are, the better society functions. Whether this is the most effective use, in terms of benefits to society at large, of outstanding intelligent individuals will be addressed in a later chapter.

True genius is ruthless in its pursuit of knowledge and achievement, and almost always ignores, if it does not actually defy, the social fabric and convention. To quote Van Tassel-Baska (1989):

> The characteristics that separate the eminent from the merely competent are a driving desire to succeed and an ability to break out of old patterns. Within eminent individuals there exists an urge not to settle, conform or become complacent; a zeal to continue the effort; and a willingness to recognize how short of the mark they may have fallen. (p. 156)

Hunter has been known for a long time as "The Genius School" (see *Life Magazine,* 3/27/48), but our interviews suggest that genius is not what Hunter wanted.

chapter 6
Women's Issues

All of the subjects, male and female, in the present study went to Hunter in the period 1945 through 1960. This period was a hiatus between the temporary liberation that World War II afforded women, and the women's liberation movement of the late 1960s. How did the subjects of our study perceive the expectations attached to gender roles during their years at Hunter?

PREVIOUS RESEARCH

Earlier work suggests that this is an important question. For example, Feldman's (1984) follow-up study of some of Terman's subjects found that women with IQs above 180 had higher career achievements than a group of women with IQs of 150. Only one of 11 women in the latter group had a full-time career, and none of the others tried to pursue even part-time work. On the other hand, one of the higher-IQ women, an accountant, did say she would have preferred to be a housewife.

In addition, Feldman reported

[In the higher-IQ group] only those who worked indicated overall life satisfaction.... For women, the difference [between satisfaction or lack of it] seems related to having some sort of job or career. (p. 521)

Schuster (1990), in her review of four previous studies (Birnbaum 1971, 1975; Ginzberg 1966; Schuster 1986-87; Terman & Oden, 1959), concluded that social context played an extremely important role in defining the opportunities and roles available to women in general and gifted women in particular. She found that with recent changes in society,

> Increasingly larger proportions of these women [i.e., gifted] are obtaining advanced degrees and are pursuing challenging careers that make use of their abilities...increasingly greater proportions of these women have been in a position to experience high satisfaction and to achieve feelings of efficacy in their careers...conditions for gifted women have improved appreciably over the past fifty years. (p. 476)

At the same time, Schuster cautioned that

> Some gifted women still are burdened by feelings of self-consciousness and social awkwardness, and...the effects of being labeled "gifted" may not be altogether positive.... (p. 477)

WOMEN AT HUNTER

In general, our exploration of women's issues is divided into several areas: female role models; sex-role stereotypes and expectations; gender differences in behavior and treatment; and influence of the women's movement later in life.

Role Models

In the public elementary schools of the time, teachers were assigned according to sex-role stereotypes. In contrast, at Hunter there were a number of male homeroom teachers, in addition to the standard male slots of shop teacher and science teacher. In spite of this fact, all but one of our respondents mentioned only the female teachers.

> I have never thought about it until this very moment, but why in the world weren't there some male teachers?...Absolutely zero males among the faculty. (Female, age 43)

> I never thought about it at the time, because that's how the world was in those days, but almost all the teachers at the school were women. Maybe the shop teacher, and one or two other specialty teachers. But almost no men. I think it affected my attitude in that I didn't until much later see men as having much to offer me, either in terms of what I could learn from them or as someone capable of emotional nurturing either. (Male, age 41)

For many female subjects, the women teachers made a strong and positive impression as role models.

There were two women teachers who were really important in my life, Dr. C_____ in AVE [Audio-Visual Education] and Miss B_____ in art. Also Dr. Brumbaugh, that she was a woman and she was the principal.... There was something austere about her and something that was loving and wonderful and intellectual, and that she was a woman made a great deal of difference. (Female, age 43)

I liked the teachers. It was really a great environment. It must have been unusually good for girls because all the girls I know who went there, none of them ended up just passive mommies. Everybody functions in a way that interests them. I don't know of anyone who's professionally frustrated after going to Hunter. (Female, age 46)

Sex-Role Stereotypes and Expectations

Just as our subjects expressed dramatically opposing views of the same school environment in terms of competition, they reported very different kinds of experiences related to gender stereotyping and expectations. For some, Hunter was a place where anything was possible for girls as well as boys. This was confirmed by the following responses.

When I look back on it, what I was interested in was when we had a subject like Sister Kenney, or Florence Nightingale. It was amazing. They were women who did things. They were nurses, and this teacher showed us these things [that they accomplished]. They became role models.... I had a lot of interest in all the women she presented. (Female, age 41)

I don't remember getting messages from Hunter that women did or did not pursue careers. There was no feeling that little girls were not as bright as little boys. It was not a career-oriented place that I recall. (Female, age 38)

I think it was my assumption as a youngster that I myself and everyone else in my class would be well-known and famous. It took quite a while for me to figure out that this was not necessarily the case. (Female, age 46)

Others found a subtle refinement of the prevailing attitudes of the time.

I remember filling out a questionnaire at Hunter for Dr. Brumbaugh, and being a female I could have chosen to be a teacher or a nurse. And that was the expectation in the fifties, being a female.... I ended up being a teacher and being a medical assistant.... I had accomplished that and then I went on to do new things that were being offered in the world to me as a person. (Female, age 43)

Many women, not just our Hunter subjects, experience a conflict between the ideas of career and achievement versus motherhood and family. It may be a more pointed conflict for the Hunter subjects because in general they were told that their intelligence was a valuable resource that was not to be "wasted" in nonintellectual pursuits such as motherhood. Those subjects who discussed this area did, on the whole, find ways to include both.

> What I wanted out of life when I was at Hunter was to be a doctor, and I didn't really think about anything substantive other than I'd be a doctor, a good doctor. As soon as I got to junior high school, and my grandmother died, and I became pubescent, I began to think that all I wanted to do was get married and have children....So I basically gave up any of my career plans because that was something that was of overiding importance. (Female, age 49)

> My goals have always been to be married and have a family. Very traditional, simple goals, and I haven't achieved those goals. I don't think they have anything to do with my experience at Hunter Elementary School....I was of that generation which assumed that you worked for a couple of years until you got married....My choice of a career, up to that point, was never viewed as primary income—that I was going to have to support myself.... But I didn't think when I was married either that being a full-time housewife would be really enough for me either. (Female, age 44)

> I remember being specifically embarrassed when I was younger to say that I wanted to be a wife and mother, because I thought that wasn't enough. I felt that somebody had to love you and choose you, that kind of goal as opposed to being a doctor or a lawyer or something. (Female, age 43)

> I worked for eight or nine years before I what I call "retired" to raise my own children. I stayed out for a number of reasons. Both professionally and personally I felt it was very important to be home when the children were small, and I was able to be home with them. (Female, age 45)

For many women, it was the family, not the school, that determined the values and expectations in this area.

> My answer has nothing to do with school, but with home. My mother taught me how to cook, and girl's stuff. I can't remember her ever saying, "Well, I'm teaching you this so that you'll be a good wife and you'll find a husband and stay home and have two children." She taught me that stuff because you ought to know how to make a lamb chop for yourself and sew on a button. Because it's easier than trying to find someone to do it for you....She worked and she prepared me to go out and earn a living and be an independent adult person. I could always imagine myself in the

board room of Chase Manhattan Bank, but I was never able to come up with a picture of me wearing an apron in the kitchen in the suburbs with children. What I imagined for myself was being a sort of self-supporting independent person in some urban area. And that's what I am. (Female, age 39)

I'm in that funny generation of women that got stuck between the two sides of society. We were brought up, despite the high IQ, to expect that we would be married and have a family, and despite whatever we might do professionally, that we would be taken care of by some man. (Female, age 47)

Our female subjects all seem to have tried very hard to accommodate these two sets of expectations.

It's hard to say if I would have done anything differently in the professional area, because I did things in order. First I got married and had children and stayed home with my children. Then I went back to school. So all the time that other people were advancing in their professional life, I was home with children. I will never get where they are, probably, and sometimes I regret that. On the other hand, a lot of people who tried to do it all simultaneously didn't do very well at either, or at least didn't do very well by their children. (Female, age 48)

I married very young, had my children young, and lived abroad when I might have been establishing a career, and sort of settled into a type of life that is not very different from that of the generation before. It's very different from what's coming up the road. So if I were to look at today's young woman and say, "Gee, I wish that were me," I would be very frustrated. But I'm not, because I don't know how they're going to do all the things they're trying to do. (Female, age 48)

Gender Differences

For many female subjects, attitudes at home undercut what Hunter was trying to instill.

With me, because I was very shy, my parents would say, "Well, it doesn't matter that you're not as bright [as your brother], you're very pretty." ...In spite of that, they may have felt that women should go into equal fields. If I had said that I wanted to be a doctor or a lawyer, that would have been fine with them. (Female, age 40)

I am the eldest daughter of upper-class European Jewish immigrants. In sum, what this meant was that while my brother was "to become," "to achieve," I was to marry well. In fact, I recall my father saying to me, "You take your identity from your husband." I did the required thing, marrying a doctor from California....And it took me a long time to become a doctor myself—I obtained my Ph.D. at 44....I think my parents were very ambivalent about having a very bright daughter, and they did not know how to facilitate my growth, since they were burdened with a value system that favored male accomplishment and required women to remain in the background. (Female, age 43)

For others, society in general seemed to contradict the values Hunter was promulgating for women.

You always have the feeling that there's something wacko about a bright girl. You feel left out. You take special steps to guard against that happening. I was very much bent on having my own family, preferably with a lot of children to keep me company. As I became older this goal became quite important....It would have been very easy for a girl of my generation to have had no career at all, or doing something dumb or silly, like turning into a suburban lady, or marrying the wrong person. One way or another there's a lot of opportunity for disaster. (Female, age 46)

What I would like would be to live in a society where I wasn't stigmatized so much, especially as a woman. I hate having to hide my intelligence. I hate having to gaze at men adoringly when I know that what they are telling me is inane. (Female, age 44)

Effect of the Women's Movement

Helson (1990) discussed the various influences on creative women, and suggested that there is much less social pressure on women to become independent. She also noted that most women who have children do so in the years when men are building their careers.

For most of our interviewees, the women's movement came too late to significantly affect the choices they made themselves. But we do see its effects on the hopes and aspirations they have for their daughters and the other women who follow.

I've tried to instill this in my daughters, that women have to be prepared today, and men as well, to be independent and support themselves. The whole society has changed so alarmingly and so dramatically. I was quite fortunate that I had the educational and personal background that led me to a very large and encompassing and quite interesting career. But the goal is to be prepared, to not sit around and expect that someone is going to take care of you, because that is absolutely not in the cards, and probably shouldn't be in the cards. (Female, age 47)

It's hard to stay married in contemporary society. This stuff is difficult, it's not easy. One always thinks that it was easier for Mommy and Daddy. (Female, age 46)

I have struggled over the years with a kind of dependency, and for a long time was very dependent. I don't know if that had anything to do with being lost in the suburbs, but I was very dependent on my husband. I didn't do a lot of things without him....I didn't have a sense of independence. I've really struggled with that in the past two or three years. (Female, age 45)

Related Issues

One subject reported feelings of competitiveness with other women in the intellectual area.

I'm not content, and this is a rather unlovely trait, when I see someone who was stupider in my class, particularly if it is a woman, I don't feel rivalrous with men at all—they can go on to become Nobel Prize winners and it's fine with me—but when there's a woman who was in my class, who was not as bright as me, and I find out that she's just published a book that's been accepted by the Book-of-the-Month club, or got an award, or something like that, I feel mildly discontent with my own life for a couple of hours. (Female, age 49)

Another woman still struggles with the old stereotypes.

I think of myself as being at one extreme: a stereotype of the often female person who's terrible at math but good at English, part of whose brain is well-developed and the other part is terrible. I feel very lopsided. (Female, age 38)

Finally, one woman discussed getting in on the beginnings of the women's movement and the consequent effects on her life.

I entered law school at the time when women were just starting to go to law school. If I had taken some time between college and law school I might have found other things to do that would have been a better match of a career. I like my job...it's a good all-around profession to be in. But did I ever say that this was where I wanted to end up? Probably not. Life's much more accidental than that. (Female, age 38)

What we extract from these interviews is that, for most of these women, the prevailing social pressures and expectations did shape their own ideas of what was possible and necessary professionally and personally. Women's roles were very clearly defined in the era in which these women grew up, and for many, the possibilities that Hunter presented were in conflict with what they were being taught everywhere else. In spite of that, they seem to have made room for both family and career, and most appear to feel that the difficulties they underwent to achieve that balance were worth the effort.

chapter 7
Living Up To Expectations

In *Educating Gifted Children at Hunter College Elementary School* (1952), Hildreth and Florence Brumbaugh, the principal of the school, said, "The Hunter staff has endeavored to develop a program which will aid the intellectually gifted to achieve socially useful and competent personalities....The aim is to create a balanced life at school that provides for complete living instead of one-sided academic living....A well-balanced personality is the ultimate goal" (pp. 42-43). They also wrote

> Past efforts in educating the gifted have been at fault in emphasizing intellectual development, the abstract and the academic, textbook work and classical studies, at the expense of the child's social, emotional and physical development....As a result of narrow training, the gifted person may take refuge in an ivory tower or find himself unfitted for effective social living. (p. 47)

The *Life Magazine* article on Hunter (March, 1948) entitled "Genius School," said

> The school's big problem is to hold its students back so that when they graduate they will fit in with ordinary children about their own age....Hunter students know they are smart, but they are more humble than cocky about their intelligence....Although their interests are advanced, their plans for the future have a refreshing normality. (p. 115)

Contrast this to the research literature describing truly eminent people (Albert, 1975; Bloom, 1985; Ochse, 1990) which describes their subjects' extraordinary commitment to and passion for their creative

75

work. For example, Bloom and Sosniak's (1981) subjects had, by the age of 35, demonstrated the highest levels of accomplishment in six specific fields. They wrote, "In most cases they gave as much time to their talent as they did to all of their school and related activities.... They lived and breathed their talent development. It determined their companions and the activities they would or would not engage in" (p. 92).

As we will see in this chapter, the now grown-up Hunter students we surveyed have for the most part achieved an impressive degree of success professionally and socially, but have not yet made a profound impact in any field of study or practice.

Recall that over 51% of Hunter men we surveyed were either lawyers, physicians or college professors. An additional 20% were miscellaneous professionals such as dentists, psychologists, authors, editors, journalists, actuaries, and accountants. The women's career choices tended most heavily toward teaching and miscellaneous professions, including authors, editors, and advertising and business executives.

We asked our interview subjects several questions about their aspirations at various stages in their lives, including what specifically were their goals and how close they felt they'd come to achieving those goals. Only a few acknowledged having had any goals.

> I think I very early on recognized that I was not destined to be a lawyer or a doctor or a person in academics, and I think I wanted to find the position where I could take advantage of my ability to understand a situation, react to it, react within it, creatively change it. I think I saw myself as somebody being involved in a business where I could relate to people, where I could try to sell them myself. And I think my life direction took very much that course.
>
> I kidded about being in politics. I think if my life had taken a slightly different turn, I might have ended up in that bent. When I attended the reunion three years ago, I quickly realized that among twenty-five or so other men there, all age 47 or so at the time, that, with the exception of a half dozen, they were all either doctors or lawyers or anthropologists or poets and they truly did follow very much more intellectual pursuits. I kidded the others that I was the only one there that could sell everybody something. (Male, age 49)

> When I was young, I wanted to be a research chemist. Instead, I became a surgeon. I'm really clinical, I don't do much in the way of research. I think probably as I get older and near retirement, I would like to do a little more basic research than I'm doing now. I'm not far away from achieving my goal, it is within reach. I have little problems like having to earn a living, having to send kids through college and things like that, which puts a damper on my free time a little bit, but I'm not far away, possibly within sight. (Male, age 49)

I wanted to be a stage director, and it became more focused and I wanted to be an operatic stage director. And the goal wasn't realized. I had constant struggles with my parents. My parents refused to support my education in that area, so I had to go to a liberal arts school and then, I still feel, I got sort of sidetracked into things like philosophy and I think one of the regrets of my life is that I [became a psychoanalyst and] wasn't able to persist in the area that I was most interested in, which was theater. (Male, age 44)

Far greater numbers said they'd had little or no motivation at all.

I didn't really have any goals. I was not a very motivated kid. (Male, age 39)

I had no life goals. None. I had no idea. My parents said, "You're gonna be a doctor," so when people asked me I said, "I'm gonna be a doctor." (Male, age 43)

I'm not sure I really have goals in that sense. I think to some extent becoming a lawyer was sort of accidental, it was not really a very planned kind of thing. I like my job, I like the people I work with. It provides a lot of both personal and career flexibility because I can take sabbaticals and leaves of absence. There's always a job to come back to. (Female, age 39)

Some showed clear signs of feeling guilty about their lack of goals both now and when they were younger. One said

• I can't think of any, and to this day, that's something I have trouble with. I don't think I was ever goal-oriented. Right now, I have a very limited goal. I want to do a decent job, with as little aggravation and get the fuck out after work and enjoy other things like swimming, and traveling, and listening to music, and women.
  People were always asking "What do you want to be when you grow up?" and I have a very close uncle who's a medical doctor, and I always said, "a doctor," and I never even had crises of this or that or should it be something else. It wasn't brainwashed into me but I always said that without even thinking about it. Maybe I should have done some thinking about it, because now here I am—big deal. I'm not burning up the world and it's not overly satisfying. It's just the way I approach it—it's just a job, rather than a career or a calling. That's my own psyche, that's not Hunter, I'm sure. There are those who know my capacity and my background and say "C'mon you should be...." (Male, age 49)

I think that the luckiest children are the children who have a strong passion to do something and are driven or animated by that passion. Perhaps not as children, but perhaps as teenagers or very young adults. I didn't have that and that is one of the regrets of my life. I felt that was not in me, and that's why perhaps I prized so highly what I imagined existed in other people.

I would like to continue to practice my profession (lawyer) with a reasonable amount of success both financially and in terms of standing with other members of the bar. I would like most of all to see my children develop, I would like my wife to thrive. My wife is an attorney and she's in the last few years embarked upon a program of her own....I'd like to see her meet with success there. And I'd like to see my children have their lives animated early on by the kind of striving that I think was missing for me for many years.

I can only say to you that I'm not unhappy with where I am. I don't mean that I'm complacent or that I'm exhilarated, but I think I've gone further than I would have expected, and I don't mean only in the financial sense, I mean in a broader sense. I think more has happened, I've done more, I've had better relationships with my children...things like that have been better than I might have suspected they would have been if you had asked me this twenty years ago. (Male, age 48)

This is a terrible thing to say, but I think I'm where I want to be— terrible because I've always thought there should have been more challenges. I'm very admired and respected where I work, and I do very well there. I don't want to be a senior vice-president, I don't want to be president of the bank. That doesn't interest me. I don't want to devote that much of my energy and time to my job. I want to have time to spend with my family, to garden, to play tennis, and see my friends and read and find other things to do. I'm very happy with my life. (Female, age 38)

How close have I come to achieving my goals? You should never say those things out loud. So far, life has been very good to me. I've tried to help it along. I think most people who are in my situation should be very happy with where they are in life, but there are a lot of people out there who would be very unhappy being me. There also could be a lot of hidden desires to be something that I am not, which would make me very frustrated, but there aren't. I never really saw myself in career terms particularly. (Female, age 48)

I wanted to do what society told me to do, which was to get married and have children, and I did that, and I'm quite satisfied with that aspect of my life. In order to do that, I put other aspects on hold.

On paper it sounds as if I've achieved my goals for the most part, but one thing that my upbringing and Hunter did for me, and to me, was to set up impossible standards so that I constantly find that what I do is much more readily acceptable to other people than it is to me. I'm frequently surprised at how little it takes in my own terms to satisfy expectations and requirements. I am never satisfied. This is a problem for me. (Female, age 48)

Equally lacking in ambition to achieve career greatness were the many others who stated, often in strikingly similar terms, that their goals were simply to enjoy life.

I wanted to have fun. I wasn't exactly tied to the plow and Hunter did very little to convince me that was the way to go. Now, of course, there's a certain amount of adult perspective on just being happy, now I'd like to have a sense of success and self-worth and also a sense of participation with others and that in one way is expanding. This goal of feeling comfortable in the world around me. I don't want to set the world on fire any more now than I did then and I don't really need to discover a new microbe or a cure for cancer in order to feel that I'm a worthy person. I feel satisfied with my life. I feel I've handled its ups and downs rather well. (Female, age 38)

I always wanted to have fun. I think my main goal in life from the moment I was born was "How can I have a good time?" Hunter afforded me this because the things I was learning were very enjoyable. As soon as I got out of college my goal became finding what could I do that I could enjoy but still make money at, and I have been consistently able to find things. I never wanted to be rich, although it now looks as though I might be, which is strange. I've sought out a way of living that is comfortable. I've always made a game plan of where I want to be in five years from whatever the point is that I'm making the game plan from and it's worked out pretty well. (Male, age 38)

I wanted to be happy and I wanted to be successful. I wanted to be very well-read. I'm happy and successful. Maybe I'll be well-read someday.

I had no intention of being a lawyer. As far as I was concerned, I was going to be a musician, a writer, I'd get my law ticket, the Viet Nam War would be over, I'd buy my motorcycle, then I'd be gone, a motorcycle hippie traveling around the world. I really wasn't interested in pursuing law. I took that job at Legal Aid...because I needed some money...and it was a good place to work, and falling into that and liking it and pursuing it to where it has gone today, that was just a fluke. Successful was never, in my mind, high economics. Successful was being great at what you were selecting. So that was never really a goal in a sense.

If you ask me how my goals have changed today, well, today because I'm wrapped up in the typical "Marxist with the lawn" philosophy. Once you get the lawn, whether you're a Marxist or not, you need the lawn mower, or you don't have the lawn any more. Now my goal is to continue to be happy and successful. And I want my family to be happy and successful. And in terms of what I want to be, I'm very happy with what I've turned out to be in my profession and now, I'd just like to maintain it. I don't know if my goals have changed. I think my goals are pretty much the same in that sense. (Male, age 41)

What I really was looking for, from the time I got out of Hunter until I married my present husband, was someone to love me and for me to love. And it seemed like the way to find that was to be married and to have a family.

The one goal that I still have, I think, is I would like to write a novel.

My husband and I have written books together, non-fiction history books, and someday I would just like to sit down by myself and write a memoir or a novel. I'm still extremely interested in medicine and I certainly have not become a doctor. I'm 50 years old, I couldn't go back to medical school now even if it were possible, so I haven't reached that goal at all. I haven't written my novel so I haven't reached that goal either. I haven't reached any of my goals really. But I did finally, as far as this was the goal, I did finally meet somebody whom I love, who loves me and we've had an enriched emotional life together. If that was the important goal when I was 13, I've certainly reached that goal: the emotional goal of being with a man who loves me. (Female, age 50)

Although most of those whose goal was emotional satisfaction felt they had succeeded, some did not.

I think I have fundamentally the same goals that I had when I was younger. Some of them I have achieved...observing nature, and some writing and so forth, but I don't feel that I realized them nearly as much as I would have liked to. I also wanted to be a happier person, a more socially successful person, and I don't think I achieved that. (Male, age 40)

I always wanted to do something in art. I always was drawn to it and I did it in school and in high school and I started to work in advertising when I was still in college and I was sort of always fascinated by ads in an magazines. When kids were collecting trading cards, I was collecting ads—stormy pink and cherries in the snow—and stuff like that. So I think that I have always been on this track, a combination of art and commerce. I always wanted to live very well, comfortably and in an aesthetic environment. And that takes money. So I think that's why I gravitated towards advertising, where you can make money with art, not just be in a studio creating art in a pure sense.

My other life goal was to—this sounds very simplistic, the unconscious part of it—any child, any human being wants to be happy and to fit in. I wasn't able to fit in and still have a lot of problems with it. I don't think that I've achieved that as well as I would have liked to. I'd like to find a group of people that are achievers like myself, that are interested in the same kinds of things that I am. I haven't lived my whole life in New York, I lived in L.A. for about eight years, and it was always a struggle to find people where I could fit in. Fitting in with your normal average person is not easy because you have to shut off a part of your brain, and yet nobody wants to be isolated and I don't either. I haven't really achieved that. (Female, age 49)

I have always had the same life goals and I haven't achieved them. They are not goals that you—well, they have always been to be married and have a family. Very traditional, simple goals, and I haven't achieved those goals.

I got married when I was very young. Too young, too inexperienced, it didn't work out. And I haven't been able to get remarried, for whatever reasons. I can really say that I never had strong professional goals. I did have a very strong desire to be a Jungian analyst, and that was the only career that I was truly passionate about, and I wasn't able to do that. On the other hand, I have never liked working full-time. I would love to work part-time. I still feel that way. I do not like working five days a week. I just like to do other things. (Female, age 46)

Independence and a life filled with a variety of experiences were very important to many.

I have a memory that I'm really fond of. I don't know what age I was then, but it was definitely at Hunter, maybe in the 6th grade, when we were discussing professions and stuff. I remember saying I was determined not to be trapped in a prison for the rest of my life, and what I meant was the 9-to-5 world was a prison and I was not going to work in an office and I was not going to submit to this message that I heard partly from my mother: that you can't always enjoy yourself, life isn't a bowl of cherries, and you have to compromise, and all that. I was clearly seeing that society was trying to brainwash people into thinking that they had to be in prison.

I remember saying I know that there are other ways of living and that there are other offbeat professions that nobody tells you about but that if you are really resourceful and imaginative you can find them. I wanted to have beauty around me. I loved nature and loved art.

In some respects I've done very well. I have not succumbed to "prison," I'm not in "prison," and I've never been for more than six months at a time. I have certainly lived surrounded by beauty and I basically managed to create a life for myself in which I've had a lot of time to develop myself. (Female, age 42)

I have one of those phonograph records that you used to be able to make in an amusement park when I was a kid. I was about five or six and my cousin, who's quite a bit older, asks me on the recording what I wanted to be when I grow up, and I answer that "I want to be an everything man." I played it about a year ago and realized that's what I've done. I've had several careers and done well at all of them, and that's really what I meant then: I didn't want to be limited. So I guess I've achieved that goal. (Male, age 49)

I pretty much control my destiny and that's important. (Female, age 47)

I'm still evolving, which is nice. Once I achieve my goals I create new ones, because otherwise I think I would feel old. I feel that in my present position I have the opportunity to be at the top of my field if I wanted to, but sometimes I think, who cares? I mean sometimes I wonder if its important to anyone that I'm studying whatever I'm studying, anyway. It would be a lot easier to be a medical researcher or something in that light. It would be easier to rationalize. So my goals...I am ambitious and I want to have an exciting life, and I think I have a fairly exciting life, and I am achieving well. I'd like to get married at some point. I'm not yet. (Female, age 39)

One respondent gave a particularly interesting view that seemed to sum up the feelings of many others. For this reason, we quote her in some detail.

I think it was my assumption as a youngster that I myself and everyone else in my class would be well-known and famous. It took quite a while for me to figure out that this is not necessarily the case. I was going to be a famous lady of letters, I believed.

I had a drastic lowering of expectations, but I guess I'm not too far off the mark. You become more realistic, but basically not too different, all things considered. Essentially we were a bunch of striving little kids and one was expected to carry one's weight somehow or other.

Of course, as an only child I was very much bent on having my own family, preferably with a lot of children to keep me company. As I became older, this goal became quite important. Security, family is extremely important.

The part about money had not occurred to me until recently, that that is a very valid goal. I wish I'd thought more about it earlier. How I could have spent so much of my life, say the first half, in a state of total anti-materialism is unclear. But somehow I did not tune in to the truly significant. I've been tossing it around the past year or two, thinking that I might have plotted things out in a slightly more profitable fashion. Of course, I regard this as a low-down sort of thought.

I'm medium satisfied. I'm very happy with having the sense to become professional at all, and have a career at all. I think I could have done better if I had been more ambitious at an earlier time, if I had my priorities straight, if I had my goals lined up, if I had behaved more professionally when I was a younger person. I could have realigned things. I went through graduate school in sort of a casual manner, thinking it was all my just due, and not taking it as seriously as I should have. I was very bent on having children and threw myself into that when perhaps I should have again been behaving in a more professional manner. Year by year there are little changes. I'm still tossing it around. Perhaps tradeoffs aren't necessary and if I had a more powerful personality, more authoritative personality, more demanding personality, I could have pushed my way ahead in all directions a little better. Nonetheless, I'm pretty pleased. It does seem to me that everything that I have achieved, modest that it is, was extremely consciously done. I wonder if that's true with other people. I wanted to do this, I wanted to that, I did it. There was not much casualness or devil-may-care attitude. In general, they were the right choices. What I'm thinking of particularly is that it would be very easy for a girl of my generation to have had no career at all, or do something dumb or silly. As a young person I was extremely prone to doing something dumb or silly. I just never had the opportunity.

You asked, if I could have traded in all of the family life, etc., and gotten in return for that, the opportunity to be the preeminent historian or whatever, with Pulitzer Prizes lining the wall, and a household name, would it have been worth it? Probably not. I simply cannot imagine charging through life alone. (Female, age 46)

Some of our subjects wish they had had more motivation. At least this was suggested by their responses to the question, "Looking back on your life now, do you wish you had done anything differently in your efforts toward occupational and social achievement?"

Yes. I wish that I had more of that sense of being driven, not to the point of madness, but all of my children seem to me to have a stronger sense of themselves and to be much more willing to articulate what they'd like to do, both short range and long range. (Male, age 48)

I wish I would have been a little more academically motivated when I was younger. I was bright, but somehow, after Hunter and later years, school did not interest me that much. I did well, but I didn't get out of my education as much as I would have liked to. I would like to have learned more, I would like to know more now. I cherish learning now more so than in the past, but that had something to do with the way schools are structured.

I don't regret not being more focused earlier because I'm very process-oriented. We have to find our own way to our own experiences. I'm not satisfied with who I am, I'm not satisfied with everything I've done. But I don't regret anything, except for not being more focused on learning. (Male, age 38)

I think one thing that I regret is not having tried harder to enter and compete in the college environment. And yet I very clearly made that decision because I was tired of being singled out as intellectually gifted. That, I would change at this stage. Occupationally, I feel satisfied where I am. I think I made some good choices. Perhaps it would have taken me a little shorter time to get there. (Female, age 38)

I wish I had more school earlier, so that if I wanted to change careers, I wouldn't really be starting from scratch, I'd be starting halfway through. I'm not sure that I want to change careers, but it is an option for me. And I'd like to have that option. I'm doing OK. I'm doing better than most people. (Female, age 39)

I really like what I'm doing now. I feel very fortunate. In some ways I have very few regrets. It took me a long time, though. I had a very prolonged period of "what am I going to do when I grow up?" probably beginning at age 18 when I went to college and not ending till I was about thirty. It would have been nice to have had more direction younger, and yet look at the people who are coming out of college now and know that they want to go to business school and make a million dollars. I don't envy those people especially. It seems as if the whole thing was long and drawn out in my case. No one ever said to me "Decide what you're going to do." (Female, age 38)

I wish that I had been forced into an educational circumstance that would have forced me into learning more how to study seriously, how to be a little more analytical in educational studies, maybe gone on to be a lawyer, put all of that into my pocket and then go on to do exactly as I did, but have the knowledge of a more structured pursuit where I set out to do something very strongly and had the comfort and the reward of having succeeded in it. I should have been more serious about the whole thing, even if I ended up in the same place.

It's funny, I clearly know that lots of people would trade positions, because I have reached a level of comfort and I live nicely, and I certainly have nothing to complain about. Other than the disruptions in my life caused by marriages, I've always been very happy, and I've been very successful, and I've always considered myself to be extremely lucky. And yet there is this underlying frustration that somehow or another, there should have been a greater degree of success. That's a little bit of a contradiction, so I voice it a little timidly because on the one hand I'm perfectly satisfied and on the other hand I think that I should have pushed myself harder. (Male, age 49)

Others expressed regret that they had not been sufficiently practical in their decision making.

I wish I had tempered my intellectual/social nonconformity with a little more practicality. I spent a lot of time as a "back-to-the-lander," a rural dropout, and when I found that wasn't satisfying anymore and returned to a more conventional lifestyle, I found myself definitely at a disadvantage in the job market, being 10, 15 years older than the people I was competing against. That doesn't put you in a competitive position. (Male, age 42)

Well, I guess I would like to do it all over again knowing what I know now. Sometimes I think that it might have been nicer had I just done something like go to business school, get a nice business sort of job, earning a quarter of a million a year and do "the string quartet thing" on the side, symbolically speaking. I assume most people would like to have another shot at it. (Male, age 44)

My educational goals were fairly confused. I don't blame that on Hunter at all. If I have anyone to blame it on, it would be that my parents, primarily my father, didn't give me a clear picture of what the working world was like and what goals might be realistic. It was assumed that since I had a lot of talents, I would find what I liked. It was left up to me. I was a sociology major for a while, and a math major, and I considered a double major in psychology, and picked up computer programming along the way, and drifted into one job or another. Those jobs were supposed to support me while I wrote the great American novel. I wrote a novel. My career goals were not very realistic. If you look at my resume, it all looks like it was planned and very sensible, but that's all skillful arrangement of the facts. I'm not sure how much I would have done differently, but I think that if I had understood the world a little bit better, I would have been less confused as to what would have been sensible to pursue and what would be the results of pursuing one thing or the other. (Male, age 38)

On the other hand, some wish they had been less intense.

I wish I hadn't graduated from high school at 15, and I wish I had started college when I was a little older and could have done it right the first time. I'm not unhappy about what has happened, but I wish I would have taken two years off from college after my first year. Being two years younger than everybody was a real hard thing, and that happened to me from seventh grade on. (Male, age 41)

I wish that my college education was broader. That I had spent less time studying chemistry. I studied chemistry, which is what I really liked and I sort of didn't take English courses, history courses, and I sort of regret that now. It seemed like a good idea at the time and I did well in them and it wasn't a problem for me, but I just feel a little bit of a void in that aspect of my education. It was a conscious choice. I knew what I was doing. (Male, age 49)

I feel the world owes me some time. When I joined my practice, I wrote a sabbatical into the contract so I could take time. One of these days, as soon as the children get done with college.... (Male, age 43)

Over 80%, however, seemed satisfied with the balance they had achieved between drive and relaxation.

Right now, being in the middle of a doctorate, I wish I had done it earlier. It would have been nice to have this degree out of the way, because it's towards a goal of being a licensed psychologist, which takes a while to accomplish, especially while I'm working. But, no, I'm pleased with the route. (Female, age 46)

I left law school when my husband was drafted into the army and we went to Chicago and I had a baby and then I came back to law school. As soon as I graduated I had another baby, so my legal career was very bouncy and wacky. But it worked out. (Female, age 46)

I had done really well at Dalton and I wanted to go to Bennington. I had this goal in mind of going to a college that was like Dalton, which probably was a mistake. When I got there I didn't do anything and I almost flunked out. I procrastinated and I had lousy study habits. I just didn't know what I was going to do. I spent the summer painting and I saw that lifestyle and thought, "That's not for me. I think I'll do something a little more traditional." So I transferred and with luck, and by the skin of my teeth, I got accepted at Cornell, which was a good thing. Part of it was conditional on how I did on some science courses, prerequisites, and, of course, I got A's. So once I got on to a track, then I had no problems. It just was a matter of time. You know, who knows what it would have been like without the misery? (Female, age 49)

I never cared about achievement. I don't really care about it. I think if you are driven...that's fine for you. I've tried to lead a good life. Good not only in the sense of being happy myself but in an ethical way of life. I really wanted to direct movies, to write movies, but I wasn't willing to cut the corners necessary. On the other hand, it is not like I've sat around and vegetated. I have achieved something on a modest level. I've always just kind of let things happen and it's worked out phenomenally well. (Male, age 38)

I can't think of anything I regret in my life. I started my career late. I spent ten years "dropped out." But I think that was wonderful and I'm glad that I picked a career that I could start late. And socially, I don't really regret...I can't think of any situation that I wish now I had stayed in, so I don't feel regret in that way. (Female, age 39)

Most of my life I felt that I had failed to fulfill my potential (I'm very good at self-accusations) and my actual accomplishments faded into pale pastel. My aspirations, internal expectations, were painfully high and it was hard for me to value the fact that I had led a productive useful life. Today, at 50 years old, I'm relatively content knowing that in my work as a clinical psychologist I have saved a few lives; I have planted some flowers and I have raised two adult children who are neither Republicans nor holders of the dread MBA degree. This seems to me an acceptable way to use one's talents. (Female, age 50)

Occupationally, I think I have achieved a lot. I achieved recognition in my own field at too early an age. I got a lot of awards and a lot of attention when I was young and that's very hard to follow for the next 20 years. It's very difficult. But I have a lot of satisfaction and a decent amount of recognition and remuneration for what I do now. But in terms of living an integrated life with society, I still have a lot of work to do. I have a family, two children, I've traveled a lot, but the thing I'm talking about is much more important. It is just being comfortable in the environment with people...that's far from being real yet. But I'm still working on it.

If you are a perfectionist you are neurotic, and I know I am. Perfectionists set standards that are impossible for themselves, and very often for other people as well. It creates friction because many other people don't respect those standards, and they're not amused, and you're not tolerant and they're not having a good time. So, it takes a lot of compromise and you have to learn that compromise is not necessarily a bad thing. (Female, age 49)

Occupationally, I'm still not finished yet. I still don't know what I want to be when I grow up. I've tried a lot of different fields. I have no idea where the world will lead me. Socially, the things that people talk about in normal conversations bore the life out of me. And I do try to get along with everyone. I do learn from everyone but I need to reach them on an internal level. Superficial stuff just seems like a waste of time to me. I used to always think of myself as a loner but I find I'm not a loner at all. I'm a very communal person. I need time to be alone, but I also need to be around other people and I like to go back and forth. I like being a part of many different groups now, so I don't see myself as a loner, but I don't like to get stuck in any one group because that for me would be confining. (Female, age 43)

The questionnaire included an item asking subjects to rate their feelings about their present vocation. Using a rating scale of 1 = strong dislike; 2 = discontented; 3 = no serious discontent; 4 = fairly content; and 5 = deep satisfaction, the mean for both men and women was over 4.4, an extraordinarily favorable score.

When we asked our subjects during the interview whether they were happy or content with the quality of their lives at that time, the responses were astonishingly positive. Only one, a 40-year-old man in a clerical position, offered a clearly unhappy response.

No. I really couldn't say that I'm a happy or content person. My life is a lot of frustration...a lot of frustration professionally and socially, that I don't achieve the goals that I would like to, financially, professionally, in terms of my social life. I just didn't achieve the things that I would have liked to. (Male, age 40)

Quite a few were unabashedly pleased with how they had developed.

Do I think of myself as a happy person? Yes, extremely. There is little question that my circle of friends, my wife, kids, all will tell you that I'm a pretty level-headed, pretty happy person. Very stable, predictable. Very content, in a kind of chronically content way, with the normal discontents that keep cropping up. I think some of it has been hard work and I think some of it has been luck. (Male, age 47)

I'm very happily married, I have wonderful children. That turned out better than I knew to expect. And I'm very satisfied with my career, which I didn't anticipate at that point. (Female, age 43)

At this point I'm doing just what I want to do. Allowing for modifications, I'm doing what I set out to do when I was five. I'm teaching, flying all over the country, lecturing, testifying. The problem is it's a little more rushed than even I should be able to put up with. In five years I'm going to be retiring and look forward to a massive opening up of the time and a decrease in the sort of frenzy level. See, if I'm lecturing on Tuesday and suddenly a court case that I'm consulting on goes on till Wednesday, that means I can be in three states in two days. That's a kind of pressure that I would like to try to avoid. I can see the light at the end of the tunnel. (Male, age 45)

I like the quality of my life. I'm a bit too busy, but there are good parts in it. My family comes first. I don't get to see the kids as much as I like, but they're both in college. My husband and I spend as much time together as we can. I've had the same husband 25 years. Just beyond that, combining work and graduate school keeps life very busy. (Female, age 46)

Yes, I am a happy person...a content person. I absolutely like who I am. I would not choose to be anybody else at all and I like my development and I feel Hunter had a lot to do with that. It was a big piece for me. Yes, I like who I am.

The quality of my life vacillates from day to day, but if I could put together a composite of a person that I would like to be like, it would be me. And the quality of my life is very, very high. Sometimes when someone is so actualized as I am there is a price to pay for it, but I've been willing to pay the price. Sometimes it's painful not to be a part of everybody else and to have to have as much variety as I seem to need. I am rooted in myself today, and to just settle and be less, I would just find suffocating and so there has to be a tradeoff, and that I have come to accept. (Female, age 43)

One of the things that I'm doing now that I'm getting a great deal of satisfaction out of, which is certainly associated with the kind of things Hunter would encourage, is that I'm on the local school board. That gives me a great deal of satisfaction. (Male, age 44)

There aren't any things that I would change now in terms of how I live my life in the day-to-day. (Male, age 43)

The quality of my life? Economic comfort. Lovely apartment, nice car, beautiful son, house in the country, take a vacation. Successful in business. At this point in my life, I work as hard as I have to. At varying times in the past, I worked very, very hard. For the last five years or so, I have been very content to be a little more relaxed. Sometimes I leave the house now at 9:15 because I've started to take piano lessons. (Male, age 49)

Many more were generally happy, while tempering their responses. They were either embarrassed at sounding too pleased, or acknowledging those aspects of their lives which were not exactly as they would want.

My life is peaceful. Nice family and loving relationships with friends and kids, and doing what I'd like to do. I have extraordinary freedom in my life. Financially we're not constrained. We're living a fairly simple life within that...we're not jet setters! We have what we need. We have reached a nice level of comfort. Along the way we work out how much can we do without destroying the family...how much can I be gone to do what I want to do. I go to writer's conferences. It's not easy to do when you are married, but he understands and that's very nice. (Female, age 49)

I guess it is a good life because it is set up in a sort of way where I have beneficial contacts with others. Yeah, I would opt for the positive side here. I'm a happy person. A recurrent thought that I had as a kid that has dwindled away now, that ideally if you were smart as others, how can you be completely happy about anything? You have too many thoughts coming into your head. I really considered this for a great while as a youngster and finally just forgot about this particular question! Perhaps it's simpler to be a dumb blonde, but it wouldn't be as much fun.

It seems to be a quite orderly academic type of life. Order makes me happy. It's quite well-organized, pretty productive, it's a high-quality life, but how am I defining the quality? There's a little aura of genteel poverty about it, getting back to that. But I'd say the quality is excellent.

There's one thing I learned in elementary school and that's how to get along with other kids. This has been extremely useful in almost every situation. I'm able to find who those other kids are and get along with them. This is a lifelong advantage to be derived from such a nice early experience. (Female, age 46)

I think I have more than I thought I would at this age. And I'm perhaps feeling satisfied with that. I certainly would have liked to have been the first at something or the best at something. I've been neither. On the other hand, I don't think my goals ever quite aspired that high, although perhaps my dreams did. (Female, age 38)

I think on the whole I'm quite happy. There's a lot of joy in my life but, at times, I'm not content. At times I'm still searching for a further degree of self-fulfillment and self-expression that I haven't achieved yet. You know, there are a lot of things in my life that are not perfect at all, my relationships and my circumstances. However, on the whole, I have a lot of inner resources and a lot of inner peace so I'm always growing, very consciously growing. Now, the quality of my life...well, it's vital, it's certainly creative. I'm trying to do too many things at once, so it's overcrowded. It's lacking in simplicity and order that I would like it to have. That's a goal. But it's a nourishing life, a very nourishing life. (Female, age 42)

I'd give the quality of my life about an 80. I could be getting in the high 90s. I could be getting an A+. There's a typical Hunter student! That's indicative from your earliest ages if you felt you weren't doing well enough. I could live this way for the rest of my life, but would like to get more out of life. (Male, age 39)

I think I'm content, and both professionally and personally I'm happy. I don't have any major grievances or problems, everybody's got minor ones. Other than that I'm happy. (Female, age 38)

Happy. Reasonably. I have recently learned to make a number of important compromises, and that is critical to a certain kind of personal success. So, having learned those things, I think that makes me content. Once you get around to accepting that most things aren't going to work out the way you had possibly thought they were going to work out, but that you have been able to make some sort of successful compromise, I think that is a very important thing to come out with at the other end. My life is busy, very interesting, stimulating. I think that I am very lucky. I complain about the tensions and pressures of business but I have the feeling that given the way that I am, that I like it too. I think I'd be kind of lost without it. I have a feeling that when I go on from here, whatever I do next, and there will be something in, let us say the next five or ten years, I'll still do something that involves some sort of a structure even if it is self-imposed. (Female, age 47)

I'm a happy person, and reasonably content. There are things I would still like to accomplish professionally but the answer is I don't think I'm a discontented person, I mean this is something that changes all the time. Overall, not discontented. I feel fortunate with the quality of my life. (Male, age 48)

I always have thought of myself as a happy person. When I was younger I was very happy and very conscious of that. As I get older and I lose people and things in life change, and I get a little frightened for myself, there is always that aspect. But basically, if you're satisfied with your life, how can you be other than happy? I'm not satisfied with everything, but basically I'm an upbeat kind of person. I would consider myself content, even though I'm never quite satisfied. (Female, age 48)

I'd say I'm more of a content person...not a happy person all the time. I feel like perhaps I aspire to happiness maybe too much. You know, it is like I want that to be my regular tone of life, my permanent condition. I strive for euphoria. That's really my goal in life, I guess, to be euphoric! And there's always something wrong, but I relish those euphoric times. But I'm generally content because I'm healthy and I have a good job and a nice life. I wouldn't trade with anybody. The quality of my life is excellent. (Female, age 39)

I'm not trying to find myself. I'm not searching to become someone. I am someone. And I pretty much like who I am. There are aspects of my personality that could use some work, but basically I like who it is. So, I suppose I'm as happy as the next person. Which isn't bad! (Female, age 39)

I wouldn't trade in the essence of my life. On the other hand, I wish some things had worked out differently. Law is, for me, a second career. I wish I could have been successful as a professor of 16th century English literature. But them's the breaks....My parents only now think that I have done something worthwhile [becoming a lawyer]. They did not and do not respect the academic life.

I doubt I have the drive to be a superstar...nor am I sure that we need superstars. Talented people, sure. Visionaries, absolutely. But there is more than enough focus on individual brilliance in this world. (Male, age 40)

I'd like to have more money. But generally speaking, I don't feel driven by goals that I'm not able to achieve. But there's always the question "Does one ratchet the goals down to the level where they're achievable?"

The quality of my life? Funky but comfortable. Satisfying but perhaps unconventional, to some extent. Eclectic. Maybe still, not exactly self-centered, but internally rather than externally directed. (Male, age 42)

Not unhappy, not jolly. People don't think of me as jolly. I'm sort of content. The quality of my life is good, probably above average. (Male, age 49)

A few, however, expressed contentment despite significant hardships, especially financial.

I would say that basically I am a happy person, but I have had a tremendous amount of unhappiness in my life. You just happened to hit me at a very happy period right now. And I am very content with my life but there are a lot more things that I would like to do to make myself feel really more secure. There are things that are achievable, but it's going to take a tremendous amount of personal spiritual work, because they are things that are practical. I tend to emphasize art and my love for my children and my love of pleasure, which is travel, and I've led a very romantic life and all those things are the obverse of investing in real estate and thinking of your future. I mean I just became 50 and I would not say that I have a very secure financial state. I'm making a very decent living and I brought up two children but I don't have any great investments that are going to carry me through when I'm 70 in 20 years. So that's what makes me unhappy. I feel that practical skills were lacking in terms of how to create some sort of security for myself. I mean, I am really lacking in that. (Female, age 50)

I got married and had two children but the marriage was very poor and it broke up. Then I married a man with three children, and for the last 20 years, he and I have been working together and we love each other very much. We've also been dealing with the problems of having five kids, who are now grown, but it doesn't stop just because they're grown up. We also have rather severe financial problems, so any of the goals I might have had are submerged in making sure we have enough money past my husband's salary for the next year.

If you can say that all your goals, except your goal to get married, failed, and that you've been an underachiever who never lived up to her promise, and in spite of that you can consider yourself a happy person, then I consider myself a happy person, because the day-to-day makes me content. It is only when I start thinking in terms of the large things, when I look what I did with my life…but on the day-to-day I consider myself happy. Every once in a while I think things could have been different. I think to myself, "Gee, if I had become the doctor that I had wanted to be, I'd have a very high income now, forget whether I would have done wonderful things for humanity, and we wouldn't have an income problem." But on the day-to-day I'm content. (Female, age 49)

As with any highly verbal and reflective group of adults, the graduates of HCES interviewed for this book expressed a wide range of responses to the questions we posed to them. There were, undoubtedly, some HCES graduates who avoided participation in the study because they were embarrassed by their present situation. Yet we believe that our sample, one-third of the entire population, is fairly representative of the rest of the cohort. The administration of Hunter hoped to produce happy, well-rounded people who used their intelligence to enhance their own quality of life. It seems clear that, in the majority of cases, they succeeded very well. Our subjects' main motivations were, and are, to enjoy their lives. They generally succeeded in their careers despite a striking lack of passion to excel. Presumably, most worked just hard enough to reach a significant level of comfort. Even with the benefit of hindsight, the respondents generally profess to only the mildest of regrets about their lack of drive, despite its having almost certainly prevented fulfillment of the childhood predictions of the "Genius School."

chapter 8

The Education of Intellectually Gifted Children: The Day-to-Day Reality of Gifted Education at Hunter College Elementary School†

Perry N. Halkitis*

In 1950, a visitor to Hunter College Elementary School described his impression of the school as "a small laboratory of working democracy" (Brumbaugh, 1958). Three decades later, the Elementary School is still a stronghold of democratic ideals—ideas that reflect who we teach, how we teach, and why we teach. But within this laboratory, there exists the continually evolving debate regarding the actual, day-to-day practice of gifted education.

In what follows, an attempt will be made to provide a view, perhaps more of a glimpse, at the daily workings of the school. Despite the increased research in intellectual giftedness over the past 50 years,

* Perry N. Halkitis is a teacher at HCES and a doctoral candidate in Quantitative Methods in the department of Educational Psychology at the City University of New York Graduate Center

† Special thanks to my colleagues for their assistance and to Judd Greenstein and Juliet Ross for sharing their insights.

issues of gifted education are perhaps as intangible and controversial as when the idea of special education for those with exceptional intellectual ability first appeared in the mainstream of American society. Yet it is within this arena of debate, experimentation, and analysis that Hunter exists, redefining the purpose of gifted education in our ever-changing society.

THE HUNTER COLLEGE ELEMENTARY SCHOOL

Currently located at 94th Street and Park Avenue, the Hunter College Elementary School continues to function in its role as a demonstration and laboratory school for Manhattan's gifted and talented population. Observers from around the world frequently visit the school to elicit curricular ideas, and the school is used as a vehicle for research by university professors. Furthermore, in its effort to disseminate information to educational institutions, the Elementary School, along with its sister high school, publishes an annual newsletter, *Hunter Outreach,* which aims to share program ideas and innovations with administrators, professors, and other educators throughout North America.

The Hunter College Elementary School is part of the Hunter College Campus Schools, which includes the Hunter College High School, a school for the gifted ranging from grades seven to twelve. Both schools operate under the direct jurisdiction of Hunter College's Division of Programs in Education and are administered by a director; each school is headed by its own principal.

Students

HCES is housed in a structure designed to resemble the facade of an armory that exists on the site, and serves 400 students ranging from nursery to sixth grade. This number of students provides for a student-to-teacher ratio that allows for a wide degree of flexibility in meeting the individual needs of each child—a notion very much in line with those ideas of HCES's first principal, Florence Newell Brumbaugh (1958), that "Individuality is stressed within reasonable bounds by means of a flexible program." Except for the nursery class, each grade consists of two classes composed of approximately 20 to 25 students. Assistant teachers provide additional support for classroom instruction up through grade two, and student teachers from Hunter College, New York University, and Columbia University's Teachers College undertake their student teaching at every grade level.

In the last decade, the school population has more closely reflected the ethnic diversity of New York City than it did 40 years ago, when the student body was predominantly white. In formulating its philosophical objectives for 1988 accreditation by the Middle States Association, a steering committee of teachers and administrators wrote "the student body must reflect the racial, ethnic, and socioeconomic diversity of New York City" (Middle States Report, 1988). At present, the student population is composed of 23% African-Americans, 10% Asian or Pacific Islanders, 7% Latino/as, and 60% whites.

Each year approximately 1,500 students from the borough of Manhattan apply for admission to Hunter Elementary. Of those, 16 nursery and 32 kindergarten students are admitted based on procedures that reflect "efforts to draw intellectually gifted students from a broad spectrum of backgrounds" (Middle States Report, 1988). To meet this end, recruitment efforts, which include an informational night at the school and outreach presentations in various Manhattan communities, are conducted. "Equity and excellence are not only compatible, but constitute non-negotiable imperatives for the Hunter College Campus Schools" (Scott, 1988).

IQ scores continue to function as the primary selection criterion for admission to HCES, and the mean scores of recent cohorts of students match those of the graduates from the 1940s and 1950s described in this book. Candidates qualify for further consideration on the basis of their scores on the Stanford-Binet IV or the Wechsler Preschool Primary Scale of Intelligence (WPPSI). A predetermined "cutoff" score in the high 90th percentile range then narrows applicants to a smaller group for evaluation by members of the faculty and hired consultants. These second rounds of tests are designed to measure, among other constructs, flexibility, fluency, memory, creativity, and classification skills—reflecting the curricular expectations for students at the school. Based on test information, parent questionnaires regarding student behavior, and test protocols, the admissions committee makes its recommendations. At present, this committee is composed of primary-level teachers, the school counselor, the principal, and the associate dean of the school.

A crucial component of any gifted program is a strong relationship between identification, curriculum, and instructional practices (Renzulli, 1986). The definition that Hunter utilizes is somewhat directly related to the programming practices at the school. Indeed, the constructs listed above do incorporate elements of the curriculum at the school. Yet the validity of a test for such constructs at the primary level is an issue not only at Hunter but for all gifted programs which screen young students.

Teachers' perceptions and descriptions of the students at Hunter vary widely. For the most part, however, teachers would say, "They possess emotional intensity, high energy levels, active imaginations, intellectual acuity…and a sophisticated sense of humor." Teachers would also agree that most of the students at the school are extremely verbal, inquisitive, self-aware, self-regulated, creative, energetic, self-critical, and possess varied profiles in terms of Gardner's seven intelligences (Gardner, 1983). One current sixth grader is enrolled in eighth grade mathematics in the high school, while others are struggling with basic computation. Two sixth-grade students can prepare analytical essays reflecting the influence of Jamaica Kincaid's life experiences on her writing, while two others have difficulty describing a simple object in essay form. Within this broad spectrum are students who require acceleration, students who require enrichment, students who require both, students who require neither, and students who require remediation. Even within this more homogeneously grouped environment, individuals need special attention, which is provided in some form or another at the school, with the recognition that all people are not the same, and each brings to any situation his or her own strengths and talents.

Faculty

Hunter College Elementary School recruits teachers with backgrounds in gifted education or provides opportunities for the staff to study and develop methods for addressing the needs of gifted children. The efforts are regulated by a Personnel and Budget Committee (P&B) composed of the school principal, three elected tenured teachers, and a representative from Hunter College, chosen by the dean of the Division of Programs in Education. The committee oversees the hiring and evaluation of teachers using observations of instruction and conferences regarding methods, techniques, and materials. Teachers who have earned a master's degree and who have successfully completed five years of classroom instruction are recommended for tenure at the school. To assure the continual professional growth of the faculty, the school provides the staff with opportunities to study tuition free at any of the campuses of the City University of New York.

Five of the 37 teacher at the school are members of ethnic minorities and five are male. All teachers at the school possess a minimum of a master's degree; one teacher holds an Ed.D and two are Ph.D. candidates.

The sense of independence experienced by the teachers at the school allows each to follow and develop his or her own perceptions regarding the implementation of a differentiated curriculum for gifted students. Thus, a variety of pedagogical techniques, each associated with its own concept of gifted education, can be observed throughout the school. Those techniques tend to be academically rigorous, incorporating acceleration, enrichment, interdisciplinary experiences, and thematic connections. The extent to which each of these constructs is implemented varies from teacher to teacher—a situation manifested in most schools where teachers are empowered to create the curriculum. In fact, the working philosophy of the school written by the HCES faculty in September, 1991, states that "The talents and teaching styles of the faculty balance what's innovative with successful past practices, generating original, integrated and interdisciplinary curricula which are shared among educators." The curriculum is greatly influenced by what each teacher defines as gifted education.

When asked to consider the goals of gifted education, most agree that fostering of independence, creativity, questioning, and critical thinking are crucial to the program of the school—ideas supported by the research in gifted education. "The school," one teacher suggests, "is primarily devoted to developing academic/intellectual skills and problem-solving abilities." Another notes that the school aims "to teach to the highest possible cognitive level." Clearly noted is Renzulli's (1986) idea that gifted education is to provide young people with the maximum opportunities for self-fulfillment through the development and expression of one or a combination of performance areas where superior potential may be present. Tannenbaum (1986) states that creativity is synonymous with giftedness, which he defines as the potential for becoming an outstanding producer and performer, not just a consumer, spectator, or amateur appreciator of ideas. Recent efforts, including two workshops by Tannenbaum and Renzulli, have been implemented to help the staff bring the pieces of the educational process together in defining gifted education at HCES. The goal is thus to balance the successes achieved in each classroom of the school with an attempt to define the thread that connects all of them together.

Philosophical Ideals

The school recognizes that conceptions of intelligence and giftedness are evolving in the psychological and educational communities. Gardner's Multiple Intelligence Theory (1983) is, for example, reflected in the school's organization. Hunter's educational program not only supports and encourages verbal and logical-mathematical thinking, but also emphasizes musical, artistic, athletic, and social intelligences. This notion is enhanced by the belief that "gifted children are gifted all the time, and not only for one day, or a few hours per week (as in other resource or pull-out programs), and [thus] the school seeks to provide an atmosphere that is conducive to the wholeness of the children" (Statement of Philosophy). However, this idea of educating the whole child is not a new one. In fact, the course of study implemented by the school at its inception is similar to what exists today. HCES students have always studied with area specialists in art, music, science, foreign language, and physical education. It is almost as if intelligence theories have caught up with the practices at Hunter, or perhaps the way the curriculum is administered at Hunter, at least for the moment, is "in vogue."

The Hunter Community

This notion of a Hunter community can be viewed as an extension of the ideals established at the school in the 1940s and 1950s. Different causes, however, attract the students' attention today as compared to when "The School [cooperated] with the local civil association in philanthropies, the Boy Scouts and Girl Scouts, and similar groups" (Brumbaugh, 1958). The school currently has a mandate to train its students to have an impact on society (Middle States Report, 1988), yet there is no general agreement among the various Hunter constituencies about what "impact on society" truly means. Does it mean becoming doctors, lawyers, composers, painters, and researchers? Or does it mean that the school helps mold individuals who try to become "good, hard-working" citizens? We ask ourselves whether and in what ways the school is truly training children to become the kind of creative, nonconventional thinkers who tend to make outstanding contributions. In the best of all worlds, unconventional thinking and creativity will be rewarded justly; often this is not the case. Conventions and traditions are upheld even at a school like Hunter. Thus while assuring that HCES students develop thinking skills that allow them to move beyond the rules, the community is also dedicated to developing in students the tools and skills necessary to function within the constraints of our society. Ideally, the program at Hunter provides a child the opportunity to climb the educational ladder to achieve success, and then hopefully utilize this success in areas of need, such as the elimination of racism or disease, which affect our world. In the end, educating the "genius" may not be so much shaped by the school curriculum but by the realities and expectations of our society.

The Program

The philosophy of the school, as noted in a variety of documents including the Middle States Report (1988), sets the tone for the education provided at the school. But the program of the school is not carved in stone. It is not a set of skills, concepts, or attitudes covered from year to year, from grade to grade or even within each grade, with the same pedagogical approach used by all teachers. Instead, it is an essence, an aura, a fuzzy cloud, flexible and redefined at any given moment to accommodate the needs of the students. There is general agreement among the faculty members on the essence of the program conducted at each of the three levels—early childhood, primary, and intermediate. In a document prepared by the faculty and published in *Hunter Outreach* (1988), the characteristics of the three levels were seen as follows:

In the early childhood years, the program focuses on the newly admitted preschooler. Because 4–5 year-old high IQ children possess a highly developed memory and vocabulary, and advanced abstract reasoning ability, teachers at this stage encourage and foster the organization of information and the generation of ideas. This may take the form of teaching strategies that highlight the skills of classification, seeing relationships, sequencing, and metacognition. From these strategies students begin to generate their own ideas. Fragmented, disconnected, or even contradictory thoughts are focused with the assistance of the teacher. It is at this crucial stage that teachers introduce the notion that solutions or outcomes of one situation can serve as a source of new ideas with more complex goals. Children work with materials to solve questions and raise new ones. Students are exposed to the literature of authors such as E.B. White, Ruth Chew, Edward Eager, and Isaac Bashevis Singer. In mathematics, students are introduced in mathematics to addition and subtraction with numbers up to 1,000 and the logic of thought involved in the scientific method. Through laboratory experiences, children pose questions, hypothesize, collect data, and evaluate.

The primary grades focus on helping students move from developing general ideas to applying them in specific content domains. The idea of sequencing is discussed in terms of historical events or the stages of a chemical reaction. More emphasis is placed on defining and refining the student's mechanics and skills based upon individual strengths and weaknesses. Language arts, mathematics, science, social studies and all other areas of study are linked to the child's advanced vocabulary, verbal fluency, and strong memory skills. Most students at this level read well, readily process information, and can easily decode and decipher new information. Students possess long attention spans, ask probing questions, and have a good memory for concepts heard and read. Some students also begin to demonstrate strong leadership abilities and set high standards for themselves and their peers. They become concerned with ethical issues. Furthermore, there is an emphasis on research processes during which students begin to gain greater independence in learning. Writing from personal experience is encouraged as is individualized reading for pleasure and comprehension.

Classrooms are arranged in such a way as to facilitate both small-group and whole-class instruction. Vocabulary is developed from the various curricular areas. In mathematics, there is a sequential path of mastery at all levels—numeration, operations, geometry, measurement, probability, and statistics. In social studies, understanding of diversity is stressed to develop positive attitudes, through a focus on the family and communities. Because the focus is teacher-dependent, one first-grade class may be studying communities through an intensive investigation of Ancient Egypt, another through modern-day Japan. Students gain scientific knowledge by experiments which provide the basis for all concepts in technology, earth, life, and physical science.

Students carry out research and create puzzles, board games, paintings, sculptures, and songs on a wide variety of topics including Ancient Egypt, birds, women in history, animals on the edge of extinction, and measurement. Class presentations and festivals are undertaken and include such themes as a math fair, New Amsterdam Museum, and Egyptian extravaganza. The use of an artifact box helps students gain further involvement in research as they undertake an analysis of materials from a given area of the world and are asked to identify the location. Access to the library and resource specialists also function to enhance the curriculum. Students at this level also write novels, allowing the students a creative outlet for ideas, frustrations, and emotions.

The intermediate grades enhance the mentor-apprentice relationship between students and teachers. It is at this level that students critically examine their performances with the assistance of teachers. Students are helped to develop and refine strategies used in investigation and experimentation, moving through a series of steps—from brainstorming, to locating and organizing information, to creating plans for the evaluation of information and resources, based on experiences in the early childhood and primary years. Academic skills and concepts are strengthened and refined, enhancing the role of students as independent investigators. Discussions of literary works focus on the recognition of mood, plot, characterization, setting, conflict, and themes, and are incorporated in each student's analysis of the work through expository writing. Note taking, outlining, mastery of the four binary operations is stressed, and students are encouraged to explain their mathematical thinking and apply it to nonroutine situations. Oral and dramatic presentations, debates, and the creation of murals and games also function to enhance the curriculum at this level. Students are exposed to activities in the arts that call upon them to elect independent research topics using primary and secondary sources.

This general outline, while providing expectations for each level, is not a specific plan or prescription followed word for word by the teachers. The Hunter community is relatively small, and the teachers know most of the children at the school. When students arrive at a designated grade level, the incoming teacher is already aware of the skills, abilities, and interests of the particular class and can provide for curricular instruction which is tailored for them.

There are also pitfalls to this arrangement. "Gaps" of knowledge have been noted in some students. Because, for example, there has not been a particular sequence for studying history through the grades, students may never be exposed to the immigration movement into the United States during the early 1900s or the sociopolitical structure of South America. However, there are currently efforts underway to organize the basic content and skills to be studied in each subject at each grade so there is a greater sense of articulation in the curriculum. Already a sequence of reading skills has been published by the school, and efforts are in progress for sequencing skills examined at each level in social studies. The codification of skills will not confine teachers to specific content. Each teacher will continue to bring his or her expertise to a domain while assuring that the skills developed provide a foundation for the more complex skills introduced later. Regular staff meetings within the elementary school and between the upper grades of the elementary school and the high school seek ways to address these issues. Two issues that seem to permeate these discussions are academic rigor and enrichment within the curricula.

The Role of Acceleration, Enrichment, and Academic Rigor

As has been noted, a definitive instructional and curriculum model for the Hunter College Elementary School has not been clearly delineated, although it may be argued that the epistemological model (Maker, 1982), in which the teacher exposes the students to key ideas, themes, and principles within and across domains, is characteristic of much of what takes place at the school. In such an approach the teacher raises issues that lead to debate and discussion as well as future exploration (Van Tassel-Baska, 1988).

Content acceleration has been quite beneficial to the education of gifted children who may be ready to learn concepts and ideas at earlier ages (Gallagher, 1985). "I use materials intended for students in grades five to eight to vertically accelerate the curriculum," notes one teacher. "Math students basically study topics at least one year or more above grade level," suggests another. In fact, even students in the least advanced sixth grade math group utilize a seventh grade Houghton-Mifflin text.

Students in the intermediate grades also analyze literature usually studied on the high school level. Analyses of Shakespearian plays, novels by authors such as Ernest Hemingway and Chinua Achebe, and poems by writers such as Pablo Neruda and Nikki Giovanni are commonly studied on the intermediate level. Students accelerated in literary analysis may be asked to undertake a self-initiated project rather than partaking in the somewhat lower-level analysis the entire class is conducting.

Slavin's (1987) ideas regarding between- and within-class ability grouping are used extensively at the intermediate level. This is not necessarily true in the other grades, where contrary to Slavin's research and a recent statement of The National Association of Gifted Children (1992), grouping of any type is seen as having a negative impact on students' self-esteem. In addition to the use of accelerated materials, subject matter is compacted. Students may study fractions for two weeks, rather than the more typical month-long investigation. Alternatively, students may be asked to explore concepts independently, without any formal instruction from the teacher.

In some classrooms, acceleration is individualized, whereby students with particular talents, abilities, or aptitudes are accelerated in their studies. In some parts of the Hunter community, acceleration of this type is viewed as grouping and is considered detrimental to the development of positive self-esteem among those not accelerated. In such classrooms, however, it is not uncommon for students to work at their own pace through a series of programmed materials.

To others at the campus schools, acceleration takes a form somewhat separate from the materials and/or pace of instruction. "I expect a lot from them and challenge them to raise their own expectations of their abilities to learn," suggests a fifth grade teacher. "Group learning experiences enable the students to serve as mentors/scaffolds for each other—in this way the group is constantly working harder." In one kindergarten class, "when children have mastered a concept, they are ready for the next step. Many times this depends on the individual, which is why it is important to provide a variety and selection of activities which are open-ended. If a child is very advanced, he or she will be able to be challenged."

Similarly, curricular enrichment has many faces at Hunter, yet as is suggested (Gallagher, 1985) the function of enrichment in all sections and parts of the school is to develop further the particular intellectual skills and talents of the gifted child. Cooperative learning, the whole language approach, guest speakers, and open-ended activities that are extensions of classroom lessons provide sources of enrichment on the preprimary level. At the intermediate level, individualized reading programs and novel writing provide enrichment. In the fifth and sixth grades, "students are encouraged to take ideas beyond the initial assignment—their interests are channeled into new works to read or new methods for applying previously learned skills." More concretely, students are asked to establish travel agencies, create civilizations, and form literature groups to discuss independent readings. In a sense, the curriculum is enriched based on what the student wants or needs to take from the enrichment process.

Perhaps the greatest manifestation of enrichment provided by the school is noted in the myriad of special subjects available to students at all levels—science, music, fine art, studio art, computer science, and physical education. In a typical week, students interact with subject specialists for 20% of instructional time. And while the curricular specialists often supplement and extend the programs undertaken by the classroom teacher, a separate individual academic curriculum is also implemented by these subject teachers. For example, the art teachers pursue a study of Greek art in conjunction with the sixth-grade social studies curriculum. At the same time they provide instruction on the concepts of color, form, or the skills of sculpting and painting. A chess program, classical music programs, school performances, and student government further enrich the educational experience offered at HCES.

The extent to which academic rigor and high-quality scholarship are demanded at the school is unclear. Expectations for excellence in process and product are certainly evident on all grade levels. But by definition, a truly rigorous curriculum is not evidenced, for the most part, until the upper grades of the school, a time when entrance into the high school becomes an impending reality. At the intermediate level students are required to compose carefully researched papers in various domains, write exposition exploring the themes of literary works, design and conduct experiments, as well as master high-level concepts in history, science, literature and mathematics. Students are tested on their mastery. Scientific reports on laboratory experiments and research using primary sources including books, periodicals, and newspapers are also required.

Selected younger grades are academically rigorous as well. In one first-grade class, students conduct individualized independent studies in which they define an area of interest and proceed to use the techniques of a researcher to gather information. This project requires the use of reference materials and primary sources as well as contacting experts for additional support. One kindergarten class analyzes and applies the techniques of famous Western painters.

The issue of academic rigor is controversial at the school for at its core is the sense that subject must be emphasized over style (Sawyer, 1988). So too, as Sawyer (1988) suggests, it conjures up the image of the school marm who is inflexible and demanding in her approach. Jackson and Butterfield (1986) note that the needs of gifted children might be better met by programs that devote substantial amounts of time to the transmission of domain-specific knowledge. At HCES, however, style—the techniques of learning and of instruction—is at the heart of the curriculum. For most teachers, academic rigor must not be stressed at the expense of enrichment. It is believed the students may learn more if the process of learning is stressed over the content. Certainly much of the educational research published in the past 20 years has emphasized the need for teachers to consider student learning style and cognitive processes over the specific content material. And perhaps for low achieving students, too much emphasis on content is not the right approach. The question is whether the debate has the same meaning for teachers of the gifted as for the educator of the nongifted. For the gifted child, an academically rigorous curriculum may ultimately provide the motivation to achieve even more. Sawyer (1988, p. 18) suggests, "We can hope that our structures of gifted education will not dwell too long on space pets and gnomes," and further argues that success in achieving academic rigor is ultimately determined by those teachers who are rigorous with themselves— "those who know what they teach and not simply how they are supposed to teach" (p. 17).

Thus the question of academic rigor too needs to be further examined at HCES. As it presently stands, the students may receive an education that is partially academically rigorous, horizontally enriching, and totally child-centered. In its attempt to provide a healthy, well-rounded environment, the school still must grapple with issues of competition. The demand for academic rigor necessitates judgments of quality and excellence in both process and product, and this judgment entails comparisons of student performance. The rewarding of excellence at the expense of others may be viewed by some as a failure to treat all equally. At the same time, a failure to recognize excellence where it is justly deserved may deny a child the reinforcement he or she needs to take risks, redefine rules, and ultimately achieve adult success or even eminence.

The Future of the HCES Student

Education at Hunter College Elementary School is only the beginning. Most students continue their studies at the high school and eventually at institutions of higher learning. Yet early educational experiences can make or break students, and thus much of the responsibility for HCES students' success rests on the shoulders of elementary school teachers.

How well are the students who graduate from HCES prepared for these challenges of high school and later life? To one teacher, the fact that HCES students tend to become confident learners and thinkers is the key to success. Another suggests, "We give students an opportunity to work with abstract and complex ideas at an accelerated pace, which is certainly fine training for life. [But] I don't think that elementary school students are prepared to tackle the quantity of work in the high school."

Perhaps most accurately, "HCES students are problem-solvers. They can design alternative solutions and evaluate which is most efficient. They are independent and confident. They are leaders who have been allowed and encouraged to think, to challenge, and to voice opinions." The students themselves are perhaps the most equipped to speak about these issues. Thus, in what follows, two former HCES students provide their views on the subject. Although the statements of the two do not represent a scientific sample of all those who have been educated at HCES, they do reflect the thoughts of two who have recently graduated from the institution.

Hunter Elementary was a fabulous place for me. In the eight years I was there, I worked with many teachers and 50 other students. I benefited a lot from the experience. I think that the most important thing I learned was how to voice an opinion. Hardly any of the classes were lectures; almost all were discussions in which everyone wanted to participate. I was always eager to learn because practically everything was interesting or fun, such as a homework competition in third grade.

Even though school was enjoyable, it was a lot of work. There was always something to do—a long-term project or an essay. When I did my homework with friends from other schools, I realized that I learned much more than they did. I was always about a year ahead of other people my age in math and English.

As I started Hunter High School, I realized that it was not acceptable to always be so sure that what I thought was true. Along with my peers from HCES, I was very opinionated in class. Many of us have trouble dealing with adults who think that children cannot have good ideas about important issues.

For eight years, I was friends with the same group of 50 people. I don't actually remember having to make friends with any of them. Consequently, when I started seventh grade I had almost no idea how to make new friends. At the end of the year, I knew only half the grade, about 100 people. I am still uncomfortable talking to people I don't know. When I graduated 15 months ago [from HCES], I had no idea how close I would stay with some of my elementary school teachers or how important they had been in my past. I also didn't realize how much I learned. I have had trouble with math since I was nine. All of a sudden, I am in advanced math. Why? Because I absorbed so much material in the Elementary School. Seventh grade was all review for me. All in all, the Hunter experience was fantastic! Even with its imperfections, the chance to receive such an extraordinary education was great.—Juliet Ross

My experience at HCES was quite unique. I went to a school for the gifted and got A's for the entire time I was there. So, to me, the Elementary School was not much of a challenge. This is not to say, however, that I did not gain from the experience. I learned how to establish relationships and got a start to my academic career. From a social standpoint, the school was a wonderful experience. But I feel I could have gained more academically.

We started off every year with a few weeks of review and then went on to learning new material. I understand that some were not moving at the same rate as I or some other students, but all the same, it wasn't fair. In the sixth grade, we were divided into three different math groups based on skills. I was in the highest and even that wasn't satisfying because due to some of the less strong members of the class, things had to be repeated many times. This situation of three groups was only in the sixth grade, but I felt dissatisfied and most times at the school.

The academic function of the elementary school is to prepare for the high school. But that shouldn't be the case. Why not learn more than basics? Why not learn more instead of going over less? If my school is for the gifted and I and others are feeling held back, then what is there to do? I doubt that I could get by in the high school without the relationship-building I learned in the elementary school. But more could be done academically.—Judd Greenstein

These are but two opinions solicited from recent graduates, but the statements highlight the issues that pervade the school—academic rigor, the need for differentiated curriculum, and the importance of relationships and social intercourse. Students perceive and experience the same conflicts, the same unresolved issues, that the faculty and administration experience—questions about gifted education that will no doubt still be considered many years from now at Hunter and at other institutions which function to educate the gifted.

The Future for HCES

In some ways, the Hunter College Elementary School of the 1990s is similar to the one established decades ago. Some programs have remained intact; approaches that were considered successful then still have power today; and the debates about gifted education that seem to permeate not only HCES but the educational community at large remain (perhaps as a blessing) unresolved. Certainly, the research has focused our attention more closely on many of the issues that we encounter. Yet a single answer to the question "What is gifted education?" seems in some ways unattainable. Perhaps the continuous discourse and debate that exists within Hunter College Elementary School is the vital center of its existence, and in some cases, success. As we continue to look at ourselves and the education we provide, we are faced with many of the same issues that educators of the gifted faced 50 years ago—how do we provide the best education possible for this exceptional group of students?

New questions are bound to arise as we approach the 21st century. The need for a multicultural education has captured our attention and the attention of all schools at this particular moment. Gifted is not defined as white and middle class. We must consider the needs of the gifted child of color, the impoverished gifted child, the gifted child from a family of homosexual parents, and the needs of the gifted child who is also visually impaired.

The answers for educators of the gifted will not become more obvious but probably more elusive. As we grapple with these issues, two very powerful factors are sure to provide direction in the years that follow. The age of the microchip is now. The home computer is a reality. Communication with any part of the world has been simplified to a few keystrokes. We must equip our students, the potential leaders of tomorrow, with the intellectual tools to capitalize on advanced technology.

Intelligence is a phenomenon that manifests itself in different ways in different people and in different domains. We must therefore reconsider the way we measure intelligence, and ultimately, the methods we use to foster intellectual behavior.

These and other issues are debated within the walls of Hunter College Elementary School. Perhaps we will never arrive at answers that are satisfying, but in debating, discussing, and redefining, we educate ourselves and remain open to suggestions about the way we educate the gifted. Therein lies the power of Hunter College Elementary School.

chapter 9
Reflections and Implications

Hunter College Elementary School was organized in 1941 to address the needs of high-IQ children, those labeled geniuses by the media and by Lewis Terman, creator of the Stanford-Binet test. As adults, the school's graduates were highly educated, extremely bright, and professionally successful. Contrary to the expectations associated with the label of "genius," however, they tended to hold modest goals for themselves, expressing, for the most part, satisfaction with their societally acceptable life accomplishments.

Without a concurrent high-IQ comparison group, it is possible only to speculate on the role played by HCES in determining the life choices of its graduates. We would like to offer, however, the following arguments, one or more of which may explain why so much intellectual power failed to be channeled onto a path to eminence. The first is that IQ is an insufficient predictive measure of great contributions to the arts and sciences. Moreover, an educational agenda that is broadly enriched, focusing on social adjustment and well-roundedness, may be an impediment to the development of talent. In addition, perhaps it is not feasible to establish a school-based program designed for talent development. And finally, perhaps the individuals in our study, many of whom had sufficient talent and resources to pursue the path to world-class renown, consciously chose not to embark upon such a course, preferring instead to use their gifts to achieve the lifestyle of competent professionals and community members. These arguments are elaborated upon below.

IQ AS AN INSUFFICIENT PREDICTOR
OF EMINENCE

Fancher (1985) proposes that while IQ tests are only moderate predictors of conventional success in our society, they are still the best single measure available and can be especially useful in identifying gifted children from "unlikely" backgrounds (p. 148). Having a high IQ, by definition, implies a capacity for rapid and efficient absorption of information, particularly in academic settings. Combined with the appropriate level of motivation and the self-assurance gained from a background of successful school experiences, positions in a wide array of high-status fields should become potentially attainable.

According to Feldman (1984), these advantages, while "presumably contributing to well-being, optimism and confidence in this society," do not necessarily reflect "a qualitatively different organization of mind" traditionally associated with genius (p. 522). In a review of the literature exploring the relationship between academic aptitude and accomplishment, a low positive relationship has been demonstrated, high-level productivity tending to be situation dependent (Baird, 1985).

Personality variables confound this analysis. MacKinnon (1978), in his famous study of architects, mathematicians, and research scientists, claimed that the differences between those recognized by their peers as being outstanding, as contrasted with those identified as merely competent, were not due to an IQ advantage, as all of his subjects' IQ scores were at least two standard deviations above the mean. Instead, MacKinnon differentiated his noncreative from his creative subjects by their passivity and contentment. In contrast, his highly creative subjects were described as oppositional and discontented.

The literature on the development of expertise, a stage one passes through on the path to eminence, notes the special influence of motivation and drive, necessary to endure extensive training or practice. This drive is at least as important, according to Posner (1988), as special capabilities. One must demonstrate both heightened drive and talent, devoting decades to a pursuit of one's talent, even when there is no guarantee of recognition (Walberg, 1988). Cox (1926), Terman's colleague in the Stanford studies, expressed her view that those with persistence combined with high but not necessarily the highest measured intelligence were more likely to achieve eminence than those with great brilliance and less persistence.

According to Waitzkin (1988), attitudes toward winning and losing are essential to great performance. As father of a United States national chess champion, Waitzkin closely observed his son's relationship to the game. At a certain level of expertise, losing became so traumatic for his son Jonathan that the boy began to marshal all his intellectual and emotional resources to win. This drive, while not necessarily an attractive trait, seemed to Waitzkin to be a primary force in the development of a national- or international-level competitor.

It would seem that the drive to win develops in conjunction with the confidence that winning is possible. Indeed, many high-IQ students, comfortable with their intellectual agility, exhibit better self concept than their agemates (Milgram & Milgram, 1976). However, a number of other researchers have reported that high-IQ children, in fact, exhibit lower self-esteem than their nongifted agemates, particularly when students compare themselves to high-IQ peers (Davis & Rimm, 1985; Kanoy, Johnson, & Kanoy, 1980; Whitmore, 1980). According to Terman and Oden (1951), and Davis and Rimm (1985), externally based rationalizations are constructed by underachieving adults and students for the absence of the drive necessary to compete at the highest levels.

More current definitions of giftedness incorporate the abilities measured on IQ tests within a larger framework. One such theory has been proposed by Sternberg (1985). The Triarchic Theory of Human Intelligence includes the following components: the cognitive functioning of the individual, some of which can be measured by aptitude tests such as IQ; the individual's ability to cope with novelty and assimilate novel events, objects, and ideas into his or her experience; and finally, the external world of the individual, that is to say, the societal forces that shape what products and activities are labeled as outstanding in that time and place in history, and how a gifted individual maximizes his or her potential within that context. HCES graduates had the requisite IQ and exposure to many novel experiences that seem to have been well-integrated into their lives. However, they didn't choose to shape their environment, but rather to adapt to it. When asked to describe from where they derive satisfaction, HCES graduates did not mention the desire to make a mark on their field. Those who did opt to make changes in their environment did so in a way perhaps revolutionary for them, but not in an arena that has led to public recognition.

GENERALIZE OR SPECIALIZE

Proponents of general liberal education believe that children at the elementary level should be exposed to a wide range of experiences, values, and skills leading to optimal functioning in society and to self-actualization. They believe that an educational plan leading to overly specialized adults is not a worthwhile educational outcome, and consequently, specialization should not take place before college. Furthermore, some schools believe that academic pursuits correlate poorly with life success, and therefore cultivate social rather than intellectual pursuits (Howley, 1987).

An opposing view takes the position that the elementary and secondary years are critical to talent development, and that basic education should be compressed in order to provide more advanced education in children's areas of interest (Feldhusen, 1986; Ochse, 1990; Passow, 1985; Renzulli, 1986). Creative productivity in a field of study must be anchored in exposure to relevant information and in learning how to ask important questions, resting on the acquisition of a wide range of domain-relevant knowledge and skills (Ochse, 1990).

Educators must consider the balance between addressing children's general strategic and metacognitive processes on one hand and specific-domain knowledge on the other. According to the cognitive psychologists Jackson and Butterfield (1986), gifted children can probably profit, with minimal instruction, from the use of general problem-solving strategies because these are the very skills they performed successfully in order to be identified (p. 178). Walberg (1988) agrees, stating that more school time can therefore be devoted to the acquisition of scholarly levels of content knowledge.

> The results [of a synthesis of 35 post-1950 studies] suggest that it may not be critical for educators and students to cover all topics and subjects equally well, as they often try to do. Because human energy and time are finite, trying to master a little of everything (or what other people know, or what can be looked up) may hamper efforts to get at the bottom of a question, to pursue a skill to one's personal limit, to acquire exceptional expertise....Considerable research in a variety of academic, artistic, athletic, scientific, and other fields suggests that world-class performance demands intensely specialized efforts for as much as 70 hours per week for a decade. (p. 359)

Bloom (1985) suggested more specialization for those who have the talent and desire to pursue their gifts. In his studies comparing schooling to talent development, Bloom described how even the smallest indications of interest were encouraged and rewarded by parents of outstanding performers in music, athletics, mathematics, and science. Instruction was tailored to individual talent and special teachers were sought for each stage of development. Another key element of the talent development process included the chance to compete with others on a regional, national, or international basis. According to Bloom, schools can either provide flexible scheduling to foster specialization or create obstacles by demanding a full complement of courses to focus on general liberal education. Further, Bloom argues that concerns about time pressure on children, i.e. that children need a chance to play, are exaggerated, since his world-class subjects spent the same amount of time on their disciplined practice as their agemates did on TV viewing.

Gardner and Feldman designed Project Spectrum to investigate individual proclivities for talent as early as preschool. The objective of the project is to give teachers the tools to assess a number of potential aptitudes that each child might exhibit and develop over the school year. However, Feldman and Gardner have not yet determined how to foster individual children's talent once that assessment procedure has been refined. Some talents, such as sports, mathematics, and performing arts are easier for schools to develop because there are systems in place for measuring and assessing progress (Csikszentmihalyi & Robinson, 1986).

Much of the rationale for HCES's curriculum offerings was derived from Leta Hollingworth's concept of special schooling for exceptionally talented learners and was designed to provide sufficient challenge and stimulation within each age cohort to preclude the need for acceleration. Developing individual students' special talents, however, was not an integral part of the school's mission. The formal philosophy and the informal value system of HCES focused on developing a balanced program of cognitive and affective experiences.

Past efforts in educating the gifted have been at fault in emphasizing intellectual development, the abstract and the academic, textbook work and classical studies, at the expense of the child's social, emotional, and physical development.

The emphasis in elementary education has been traditionally bookish, with its main goal to teach children to use books as the chief study tool. This goal is overemphasized at the expense of learning through social contacts and creative effort. The detrimental effects of exaggerated emphasis on academic attainments are shown in the failure of children with genius minds to mature normally or to fulfill the promise of their early years. As a result of narrow training, the gifted person may take refuge in an ivory tower or find himself unfitted for effected social living.

The children enrolled at Hunter exhibit special gifts and strengths relatively early, which the school program might intensify prematurely unless rounding out and compensatory experiences were provided. If a child can already read, that is all he may care to do. If he excels at arithmetic, he may care only about increasing his skill. The Hunter teachers have avoided this danger in schooling the gifted by creating a curriculum that originates in broader objectives. One purpose in setting up an enriched program is to offset this tendency toward premature specialization which would leave a child inadequate in important areas of competency. This is essential too because home training in the main tends to accentuate special interests. (Hildreth, 1952, pp. 47–48)

The evidence upon which HCES's philosophical statements were made was based more on informed opinion than empirical data. In fact, according to our respondents, parents did not tend to emphasize special talents at home, valuing instead the dream of conventional success in the professions for their children. To this day, the support for providing a well-rounded and socially based education for intellectually and academically gifted children at the expense of talent development is equivocal (Shore, Cornell, Robinson, & Ward, 1991).

HCES provided a climate in which high IQ children could develop a perception of normalcy among their peers rather than view themselves as extraordinary. A 44-year-old male from among the study participants volunteered these remarks:

The philosophy of Hunter was to give us an enriched program. We had trips all over the city, science experiments, and audio-visual programs in such quantity and quality the ordinary public schools could never provide. But when we were in a certain grade, we received lessons of that grade. They could have taught me calculus but that wasn't in the offering. The only reason that children didn't learn calculus at an early age was that it wasn't taught. Children can pick up several languages if they have the opportunity. At Hunter the only foreign language we had was the once a week class with Madame _____. I think we should have been given a daily class in foreign language beginning in first grade.

Until I reached college, school was never my primary source of education. It's hard to say what would have happened to us if we would have received an education unencumbered by the fear of letting us plunge ahead. I don't know if we need more superstars, but as long as there are superstars we might as well have been the ones.

In order to most explicitly develop culturally valued creativity over the long term, students need rigorous exposure to the academic disciplines, opportunities for independent work, and access to experts and high-quality materials (Ochse, 1990; Sawyer, 1988; VanTassel-Baska, 1989). Children should feel free to express themselves, but in the long run, not providing constructive critical feedback and frequent opportunities to exercise self-discipline may result in lowering of expectations. Creativity is confined when the depth of information is limited and standards of excellence are sacrificed (Ochse, 1990).

EDUCATING FOR EMINENCE
IS NOT A FEASIBLE GOAL

Retrospective studies of eminent individuals in the 20th century report such a wide array of early experiences and attitudes toward school that one might conclude that there is no single instructional approach appropriate to the education of the potentially eminent. In order to support this point, Bull (1985) provides the following summary from Goertzels and Goertzels' (1979) study of 200 prominent men and women:

1. Only 39% were all-around good students; 20% were honor students.
2. 8% actually failed in school.
3. 15% had less than an eighth-grade education.
4. 49% did not go to college.
5. Only 34% were counted as in any way precocious. (p. 3)

Bull further argues that eminence is so tied into the culture of a particular era that a generic method of developing greatness is not feasible. From this perspective, gifted programs should not be expected to produce culturally revolutionary individuals. Instead, programs should serve to help exceptionally able people develop their talent to a level beyond what they might have without intervention and cannot be expected to foster geniuses from among their alumni (Borland, 1989; Stanley & Benbow, 1986).

What then can these programs be accountable for?

First, we know that significant change in our forms of life—scientific, literary, artistic, and athletic—usually derives from those who have a rigorous command of the skills and knowledge involved in those forms of activity. This is most obvious in academic fields....Thus, for want of a better description, disciplinary and disciplined participation in our forms of life rather than fragmented and generalized acquaintances is likely to produce the skills required for changing our civilization in revolutionary and productive ways. Indeed, one of the common complaints of the eminent about their schooling has been its dilletantish and undisciplined approach to what is taught. (Bull, 1985, p. 15)

Focusing on talent development at the elementary school level may be premature. Except for the rare prodigy, most paths to high-level creative work begin at around puberty, and, in many cases, great accomplishment may appear at different points in the life span (Csikszentmihalyi & Robinson, 1986). For example, University High

School, an educational institution loosely associated with the University of Illinois, graduating not more than 50 students per year since 1921, has created an extraordinarily eminent legacy. Its alumni include one Pulitzer Prize winner and 3 Nobel Laureates. All but one, however, are at least ten years older than the subjects in this study. Our study participants were identified as having extraordinary academic talent at a young age, with potential for brilliance in scholarship. While one HCES student (who did not graduate from HCES) has become a figure of political importance on the national scene, the others do not seem poised to make these next ten years their springboard to eminence.

HAS THIS GROUP CONSCIOUSLY CHOSEN TO AVOID THE PATH TO EMINENCE?

The 19th century saw the birth of modern conceptions of genius and eminence. For the first time, middle-class individuals could join an intellectual aristocracy by virtue of their ideas or creative work. The trappings of the 19th-century genius' life included vigorous public opposition to his ideas, and the need to relinquish the desire for a normal existence. Such sacrifices were made bearable by profound self-assurance and a support system centered on a powerful mentor or patron (Pletsch, 1991). The great status that was associated with the label of genius is exemplified by the following comment by Schopenhauer, himself identified as a genius in the 1800s: "Talent is like a marksman who hits a target which others cannot reach; genius is like the marksman who hits a target which others cannot even see" (1966, p. 391).

When an individual engages in work that transforms his or her field, redirecting the efforts of others in that discipline, that person can be labeled "eminent" (Zuckerman, 1977). The dynamic that leads to the fulfillment of great talent includes conducive family values, outstanding teachers, early career experiences, and encounters with mentors. How much effort one expends on his or her special talents within each of those contexts, however, plays an important role in the evolution of eminence (Albert & Runco, 1986; Csikszentmihalyi & Robinson, 1986), and a level of dedication close to obsession might best describe the commitment eminent individuals bring to their work. If early propensities are to be transformed into creative accomplishment in adulthood, the right configuration of intellectual skills, personality variables, family background, and participation in a time and place in history must converge with a high level of special talent.

In the course of his extensive case studies of child prodigies, Feldman (1986) formulated a theory of "co-incidence" describing the variables essential for the blossoming of prodigious behavior. These variables, reminiscent of Tannenbaum's psychosocial theory of giftedness (1983), are also necessary for the development of eminence in adulthood:

- personality, which includes a drive to exercise one's talent and to convince others that creativity has been exhibited (see also Simonton, 1990);
- special proclivity for a field of study or career;
- a receptive culture and time in history (see also Simonton, 1990)
- access to mentors and other resources; and
- family tradition and values (Albert 1980b; Albert & Runco, 1986; Colangelo & Dettman, 1983).

Feldman believes that the likelihood that all of these variables will fall into proper place is very small. Consequently, most people find something worthwhile and interesting to do by focusing on their general rather than specific aptitudes (p. 214). Furthermore, the effort required to express publicly one's vision is immensely difficult, particularly when there is no guarantee that efforts will be recognized or that one will meet his or her own standards of achievement (Briggs, 1988).

By 1947, Terman believed that none of his high-IQ subjects would be considered among the most eminent persons in history. While predicting advantages such as relatively high income, marital happiness, health, and stability, he deduced that ultimately nonintellective factors must be the catalyst of transcendent achievement.

Moreover, Terman and Oden (1959) noticed that many of their subjects rated integrity, friendship, family, and civic responsibility as the most important achievements related to success in life. These areas, however, are the ones most likely to be sacrificed in the process of channeling intellectual and creative efforts into the development of a masterpiece. "The gifted who are endowed with strong egos pay social penalties for appearing to be arrogant, but if they did not believe their abilities were exceptional, they could never prime themselves for maximum effort when they are called upon to confirm their giftedness through yet another extraordinary accomplishment" (Tannenbaum, 1983, p. 167).

Snyder and Fromkin (1980) have proposed a model of "uniqueness" postulating that when people see themselves as somewhat like others around them, they feel most comfortable. When, however, they feel either too similar or too different, people tend to modify their behavior so as to achieve an optimal level of moderate similarity. Yet, in order to remain independent enough from social life to sustain the necessary focus on a major creative effort, the truly creative person must feel some alienation from society (Albert, 1990; Gruber, 1980).

Did the pursuit of social intercourse detract HCES graduates from profound intellectual pursuits? Is the search for a life centered on satisfying and meaningful relationships inconsistent with revolutionary thought? Tomlinson-Keasey and Little (1990), in their analyses of the Terman data, found that the most well-adjusted and liked children in the group were less likely to maintain their intellectual skills as adults. Tomlinson-Keasey et al. (1990) speculate that this finding reflects a conscious decision by some gifted individuals to concentrate their skills on social outlets and to forgo academic achievement.

Two explanations may, therefore, arise for the shortage of stellar adult productivity on the part of HCES graduates that fit in the category of willful decision making:

* Because they were labeled as gifted and treated specially through the critical years of their childhood, there was no need to prove themselves by participating in the exhausting pursuit of revolutionary change; and
* After noting the sacrifices involved in trying for national- or world-class leadership in a field, HCES graduates decided that the intelligent thing to do was to choose relatively happy and successful lives.

Personality disposition appears to be the variable that determines the difference between eminence and mere professional competence—and personality disposition is derived from family and school values and opportunities (Albert, 1990). HCES graduates were molded by family and school values that celebrated social adjustment and standard professional success and discouraged obsessive attention to special talent or recognition.

CONCLUSION

It appears clear that we need to make some decisions about our gifted children. Should we expect graduates of highly selective programs to evolve into more outstandingly creative adults than they might have by attending private or upper-income suburban schools? Could we predict that high-IQ children will evolve into competent professionals merely from their predominantly middle-class social status? Do we educate gifted children for their own happiness, satisfaction, and moderate achievement, or do we challenge them with dissatisfaction and frustration, greater discipline, and a value system that glorifies eminence? Do we land them on the moon, or aim them toward the stars?

In a sense, we choose between the society and the individual. As we have seen, the true genius, the one who in some way transforms the world, or at the very least, his or her field, is likely to be driven, compulsive, and never fully contented. We may be enriched at his or her expense. Are we to seek and develop those who might become the next generation of social or intellectual leaders, or provide a sanctuary for children who deviate from the norm in their academic and intellectual needs? There is no correct or simple resolution to this question. Either course has merit and justification. In order to avoid promoting one course of action under the guise of the other, we need to reflect once again on our values and priorities when we make this critical choice of goals for gifted education.

Appendix A

It was a plum assignment.

Being selected to student teach at the Hunter College Elementary School in the 1950s was considered not only a privilege, but an auspicious beginning of a career in elementary education. Because they were exceptionally bright, the students of this laboratory school were highly motivated to learn. All but guaranteed an education comparable to that of the finest private schools, these students afforded the budding teacher an excellent opportunity to observe and translate into practical reality lessons taught in theory in the college classroom. The philosophies and methods of teaching put forward in the undergraduate segment of the future teacher's education would now be practiced without the constraints of courting or disciplining unwilling learners.

The student teacher encountered, for the most part, friendly, enthusiastic, and challenging pupils who were extremely receptive to learning. These children quite simply displayed a gratifying acceptance of those who taught them, creating for the teacher a sense of being both successful and necessary.

> Ellen Steckler Summers
> Former Student Teacher
> Hunter College Elementary School

Appendix B

PHYSICAL CONDITIONS—CLASS 7-8, OCTOBER 1953

I. Seating Plan

    A. Arrangement of seats—There are four rows of movable desks and chairs. Each chair and desk is suited to the size of the child. Two rows face each other. There is a clear aisle between the second and third rows, and clearance all around the room.

    B. Children with any visual difficulties are seated nearest the blackboard.

    C. Children who, when seated near one another cause a disturbance, are separated. Friends are seated near one another provided they can behave.

    D. The seating plan is good in that it sees to it that bad influences are separated. Since the seats are movable, it is possible for children who cannot see or hear during a lesson to move to a more favorable location. In this way, the possibility of a child becoming bored and mischievous is considerably lessened.

II. Ventilation

    A. A thermostat is used in the room. No formal record of the room temperature is taken.

    B. Only teacher and student teachers may adjust windows.

III. Lighting

    A. The window shades are usually kept up unless there is a glare in the room or darkness is required.

B. Teacher and student teachers adjust window shades. Later on during the term, the children will take over the responsibility for caring for the shades.

IV. Comments on Decoration

A. Drawings and paintings of the children are displayed in a section above the blackboard. There is a bulletin board outside the room for the purpose of displaying interesting pictures as well as the work of the pupils. There are many plants which are kept on the window sill.

B. There are no blackboard decorations.

V. Observations on Housekeeping

A. Housekeeping is attended to after lunch, before afternoon dismissal, and after a period of game playing or a party.

B. The children attend to the housekeeping by sweeping and picking up rubbish.

C. The room is always clean and neat. Once a month, teachers and children scrub the desks with Soilax. Floors are kept clear of rubbish by the pupils. Teachers wash the boards.

D. All supplies are kept in the closet, drawers, or bins. Teachers supervise the handing out of supplies.

VI. Evaluation of Blackboard Writing

A. The form of the writing as done by the teacher is always very neat. The teacher uses manuscript on the board since the children are just learning cursive writing. There are light guide lines on the board about three inches high so that the children writing on the board can make their letters proportionate. The size of the writing done by the teachers is large enough to be viewed with ease from the farthest distance in the room.

B. The effect of the blackboard writing on the children is good since they have no difficulty seeing the board. Because the teacher's writing of the letters of the cursive alphabet is so precise, the children evidence no difficulty in emulating this form. Consequently, the children are learning the cursive alphabet very rapidly and easily.

VII. Hygiene

A. There is no formal daily inspection; however, the teacher and student teachers are very observant as far as the physical condition of the child is concerned.

B. There is no formal two-minute drill.

C. The class has stretching exercises daily. The height, weight, and vision of the child is taken at the end of every term. At the slightest sign of illness, the child is taken to the college medical office. Children who have recently been ill are excused from physical education if they or their parents request such action.

Appendix C

OCTOBER, 1953

A. Good Use of An Approved Technique
Three reading groups are conducted by the class teacher and the two student teachers. The groups are called Phi (group with lowest reading ability), Beta (group whose reading is up to standard of grade), and Kappa (group that performs above standard of grade). Each group congregates in a separate section of the room, far away from the others. This, unlike most public schools, is possible because the seats are movable. Only one child at a time may speak or read so as not to disturb the other groups. By appealing to the group pride of the children in such matters as maintaining quiet or the moving of chairs, order is kept. The group technique is an effective one because each group is small enough to ensure individual attention for each child. Since each child has more than one opportunity to read aloud in each lesson, it is possible to diagnose reading difficulties. A reading group is a good place in which to observe personality traits of the child.
B. Good Drill Device
Cursive writing is taught using the technique of drills which are conducted as a contest stimulating interest in the children and a desire on their parts to do their best. The letters are taught according to families; i.e. l,b,f; n,v,y. Written in the cursive alphabet, these groups have similarities. The contests are held between the boys and the girls. Each child comes to the board and writes the new letter. The teacher gives one, two, or three checks

depending on the perfection of the letter. The teacher's model is written on the board for each child to follow. If a pupil misbehaves, his side gets a cross, which cancels a check. After the contest, the children are given ruled paper on which to write the new letter and the other letters they have learned. The papers are then displayed on the bulletin board.

C.   Good Application of the Principles of Educational Psychology
Sharing, which is the class name for Show and Tell is conducted every Wednesday afternoon. Every child naturally wishes to participate in this activity. Sharing affords a wonderful opportunity for every child to express himself or herself before a group. It allows the shy child to break the ice, so to speak, by addressing the class without being self-conscious about it. Sharing gives the teacher good insights into the interests of the child. Furthermore, in sharing, children become interested in new hobbies and ventures by learning the interests of their classmates.

D.   Other Routine Movements
1.   Efficiency and economy of time is evidenced in all three of these techniques. In reading, the groups assemble quickly and quietly, since the teacher says, "I'll bet the Phi's will be the fastest." Naturally, the two other groups try to show that they are as fast as the Phi's. In the drill lesson, each child is eager to write on the board, and so is ready when his turn comes.
During the Sharing period, the children are encouraged to be brief and explicit. Appealing to the pride of the child, especially in group activities, fosters efficiency and saves the class time.

2.   Time Spent Between 8:40 and 9:00
a.   Children put away their coats and hats. The boys use one closet, the girls, another.
b.   Class prepares for art or gym by putting on smocks or sneakers.
c.   Morning exercises are conducted.
d.   Attendance is taken.
e.   Daily activities are discussed.

3.   The period from 12:50 to 1:00 falls in the middle of the afternoon activities, since the lunch period is from 11:30 to 12:00 noon.

4.   Since the routine movements are well established, carefully supervised and successfully executed, there are few disciplinary problems associated with these movements. Children go to the closet by rows to avoid congestion. Sneakers and lunch

boxes are kept in special bags facilitating distribution of these items. The children line up in size place in a double line.

5. Other routine movements

    a. Passing to and from the room, the children line up in single file to discourage talking. There is a rear guard to keep the line intact.

    b. Books, paper, and tests are distributed by the teacher. Milk and soup are distributed by the children.

    c. Passing to and from the blackboard is conducted to avoid congestion. Only four pupils may use the board at any time.

To ensure safe fire drills, rules are set down early in the term. The pupils are well aware of the gravity of such rules. If anyone disregards the rules for quiet and rapid dismissal, punishment is always administered.

These outlines were written by Ellen Steckler Summers from her observations and experiences at the time that she served as a student teacher at the Hunter College Elementary School.

Appendix D

**NOTES FROM MS. M., A PRIMARY TEACHER
AT HUNTER COLLEGE ELEMENTARY
SCHOOL DURING THE PERIOD
DESCRIBED IN THIS BOOK**

In reference to special training to prepare her for working at Hunter College Elementary School:

The year before she was appointed to HCES (September 1943) Ms. M. taught a class of 3-year-old children at The Ethical Culture School. She read Hollingworth, Schwartz, and Hildreth. At meetings, Ms. M. listened and talked to some teachers who taught at the Speyer School. She took a graduate course in gifted education with Professor Frank T. Wilson and attended principals' conferences that featured special speakers on the topic. Dr. Brumbaugh, the principal of HCES, interviewed Ms. M. three times before she became a member of the faculty.

What was seen as the purpose of the school:

Fifty years ago, teachers were concerned with the "whole child," especially at HCES: a balance of physical, mental, emotional, and social being. They were concerned that each child live out his or her life to the fullest while being aware of surroundings and events taking place.

1. Enrichment: In planning work, the teachers at HCES were required to locate and have available all possible materials on various topics, using different media. The children were encour-

aged to delve into this material and share their findings and discoveries with one another in groups or with the class.

2. Skills: Skills were carefully taught and easily learned by the children. Where there was difficulty, a child or a small group was instructed, and additional materials were used to assist the children. Many times, hobbies or crafts helped the children over the rough spots.

3. Physical development: Beyond the school program, parents were encouraged to see that additional physical activity was available to the child.

4. Science, Reading, Literature: HCES was one of the first elementary schools to have its own science lab classroom. There was lots of storytelling, and children were often read to by the teacher or encouraged to read to one another.

Ms. M. reported that the teachers expressed some ambivalence about this special education. Many felt that all children should have the same opportunities and experiences as those in HCES. So-called "normal" classes could be offered similar experiences at their level of attention and interest as well as the slow learners and the late bloomers.

Ms. M. felt certain that if she were in the classroom today, her teaching strategies would be somewhat similar to what they were then. The content, she agreed, would of course have to be updated.

References

Albert, R.S. (1978). Observations and suggestions regarding giftedness, familial influences and the achievement of eminence. *Gifted Child Quarterly, 22,* 201–222.

Albert, R.S. (1980a). Family positions and the attainment of eminence. *Gifted Child Quarterly, 24,* 87–95.

Albert, R.S. (1980b). Exceptionally gifted boys and their parents. *Gifted Children Quarterly, 24,* 174–178.

Albert, R.S. (1983). Toward a behavioral definition of genius. In R.S. Albert (Ed.), *Genius and eminence: The social psychology of creativity and exceptional achievement* (pp. 59–72). New York: Oxford University Press.

Albert, R.S. (1990) Identity, experiences, and career choice among the exceptionally gifted and eminent. In M.A. Runco & R.S. Albert (Eds.), *Theories of creativity* (pp. 13–34). Newbury Park, CA: Sage Publications.

Albert, R.S., & Runco, M.A. (1986). The achievement of eminence: A model based on a longitudinal study of exceptionally gifted boys and their families. In R.J. Sternberg & J.E. Davidson (Eds.), *Conceptions of giftedness* (pp. 332–357). New York: Cambridge University Press.

Ayres, L.P. (1909). *Laggards in our schools: A study of retardation and elimination in city school systems.* New York: Charities Publication Committee.

Baird, L.L. (1985). Do grades and tests predict adult accomplishment? *Research in Higher Education, 23*(1), 3–85.

Barbe, W.B., & Renzulli, J.S. (Eds.). (1981). *Psychology and education of the gifted* (3rd ed.). New York: Irvington Publishers.

Birnbaum, J.A. (1971). *Life patterns, personality style and self esteem in gifted family-oriented and career-committed women.* Unpublished doctoral dissertation, University of Michigan, Ann Arbor, MI.

Birnbaum, J.A. (1975). Life patterns and self-esteem in gifted family-oriented and career-committed women. In M. Mednick, S. Tangri, & L.W. Hoffman (Eds.), *Women and achievement: Social and motivational analysis* (pp. 396–419). New York: Hemisphere-Halstead.

Bloom, B.J. (1985). *Developing talent in young people.* New York: Ballantine Books.

Bloom, B.S., & Sosniak, L.A. (1981). Talent development vs. schooling. *Educational Leadership, 32*(2), 86–94.

Borland, J.H. (1989). *Planning and implementing programs for the gifted.* New York: Teachers College Press.

Brandwein, P.F. (1955). *The gifted student as future scientist.* New York: Harcourt, Brace.

Bridgewater, W., & Sherwood, E.J. (Eds.). (1956). Progressive education. *The Columbia encyclopedia* (2nd ed.). New York: Columbia University Press.

Briggs, J. (1988). *Fire in the crucible: The alchemy of creative genius.* New York: St. Martin's Press.

Brumbaugh, F.N. (1958). *Hunter College Elementary School gifted children: As we see them.* New York: Hunter College Elementary School.

Bull, B.L. (1985). Eminence and precocity: An examination of the justification of education for the gifted and talented. *Teachers College Record, 87*(1), 1–19.

Chapman, P.D. (1988). *Schools as sorters: Lewis M. Terman, applied psychology, and the intelligence testing movement, 1890–1930.* New York: New York University Press.

Clark, R. (1983). *Family life and school achievement: Why poor black children succeed or fail.* Chicago, IL: University of Chicago Press.

Clausen, J.A. (1981). Men's occupational careers in the middle years. In D. Eichorn et al. (Eds.), *Present and past in middle life* (pp. 321–351). New York: Academic Press.

Colangelo, N., & Dettmann, D.F. (1983). A review of research on parents and families of gifted children. *Exceptional Children, 50,* 20–27.

Coleman, J.M., & Fults, B.A. (1982). Self-concept and the gifted classroom: The role of social comparisons. *Gifted Child Quarterly, 26,* 116–120.

Cox, C. (1926). *The early mental traits of three hundred geniuses.* Stanford, CA: Stanford University Press.

Cox, R.L. (1981). Personal, physical, and family traits of gifted children. In B.S. Miller & M. Price (Eds.), *The gifted child, the family and the community* (pp. 107–113). New York: Walker & Company.

Csikszentmihalyi, M., & Robinson, R.E. (1986). Culture, time and the development of talent. In R.J. Sternberg & J.E. Davidson (Eds.), *Conceptions of giftedness* (pp. 264–284). New York: Cambridge University Press.

Davis, G.A., & Rimm, S.B. (1985). *Education of the gifted and talented.* Englewood Cliffs, NJ: Prentice-Hall.

Eccles, J.S. (1985). Why doesn't Jane run? Sex differences in educational and occupational patterns. In F.D. Horowitz & M. O'Brien (Eds.), *The gifted and talented: Developmental perspectives* (pp. 251–295). Washington, DC: American Psychological Association.

Fancher, R.E. (1985). *The intelligence men: Makers of the IQ controversy.* New York: W.W. Norton.

Feldhusen, J.F. (1986). A conception of giftedness. In R.J. Sternberg & J.E. Davidson (Eds.), *Conceptions of giftedness* (pp. 112–127). New York: Cambridge University Press.

Feldman, D.H. (1984). A follow-up study of subjects who scored above 180 IQ in Terman's "Genetic studies of genius." *Exceptional Children, 50,* 518–523.

Feldman, D.H. (1986). *Nature's gambit: Child prodigies and the development of human potential.* New York: Basic Books.

Forrest, D.W. (1974). *Francis Galton: The life and work of a Victorian genius.* New York: Taplinger.

Gallagher, J.J. (1985). *Teaching the gifted child* (3rd ed.). Boston, MA: Allyn & Bacon.

Galton, F. (1908). *Memories of my life.* London: Methuen.

Gardner, H. (1983). *Frames of mind.* New York: Academic Press.

Gardner, H., & Hatch, T. (1989). Multiple intelligences go to school: Educational implications of the Theory of Multiple Intelligences. *Educational Researcher, 18*(8), 4–10.

Ginzberg, E. (1966). *Life styles of educated women.* New York: Columbia University Press.

Goertzel, V., & Goertzel, M.G. (1962). *Cradles of eminence.* Boston: Little, Brown.

Goleman, D. (1980). 1528 little geniuses and how they grew. *Psychology Today, 13*(9), 28–53.

Gould, S.J. (1981). *The mismeasure of man.* New York: W.W. Norton.

Greenlaw, M.J., & McIntosh, M.E. (1988). *Educating the gifted: A sourcebook.* Chicago, IL: American Library Association.

Gruber, H. (1980). Afterword. In D.H. Feldman, *Beyond universals in cognitive development* (pp. 175–180). Norwood, NJ: Ablex.

Gubbins, E.J., & Reid, B.D. (1991, April). Research needs of the gifted and talented through the year 2000. In J. Renzulli (Chair), *The National Research Center on the Gifted and Talented: Present activities, future plans, and an invitation for input and involvement.* Symposium conducted at the meeting of the American Educational Research Association, Chicago, IL.

Helson, R. (1990). Creativity in women: Outer and inner views over time. In M.A. Runco & R.S. Albert (Eds.), *Theories of creativity* (pp. 46–58). Newbury Park, CA: Sage.

Hildreth, G.H. (1952). *Educating gifted children at Hunter College Elementary School* (Reprinted 1970). Westport, CT: Greenwood Press.

Hildreth, G.H. (1966). *Introduction to the gifted.* New York: McGraw-Hill.

Hollingworth, L.S. (1926). *Gifted children: Their nature and nurture.* New York: Macmillan.

Hollingworth, L.S. (1975). *Children above 180 IQ Stanford Binet: Origin and development.* New York: Arno Press.

Howley, A. (1987). The symbolic role of eminence in the education of gifted students. *Journal for the Education of the Gifted, 10*(2), 115–124.

Hunter College Elementary School. (n.d.). *Statement of Philosophy.* Unpublished manuscript.

Jackson, N.E., & Butterfield, E.C. (1986). A conception of giftedness to promote research. In R.J. Sternberg & J.E. Davidson (Eds.), *Conceptions of giftedness* (pp. 151–181). New York: Cambridge University Press.

Janos, P.M., & Robinson, N.M. (1985a). Psychosocial development in intellectually gifted children. In F.D. Horowitz & M. O'Brien (Eds.), *The gifted and talented: Developmental perspectives* (pp. 149–195). Washington, DC: American Psychological Association.

Janos, P.M., & Robinson, N.M. (1985b). The performance of students in a program of radical acceleration at the university level. *Gifted Child Quarterly, 29,* 175–180.

Janos, P.M., Fung, H.C., & Robinson, N.M. (1985). Self-concept, self-esteem, and peer relations among gifted children who feel "different." *Gifted Child Quarterly, 29,* 78–82.

Kanoy, R.C., Johnson, B.W., & Kanoy, K.W. (1980). Locus of control and self-concept in achieving bright elementary students. *Psychology in the Schools, 17,* 395–399.

Keen, N. (1948). Genius school. *Life, 24*(2), 113–119.

MacKinnon, D.W. (1978). *In search of human effectiveness.* Buffalo, NY: Creative Education Foundation.

Maker, C.J. (1982). *Curriculum development for the gifted.* Rockville, MD: Aspen.

Marjoribanks, K. (1979). *Families and their learning environments.* Boston: Routledge & Kegan Paul.

Marland, S.P., Jr. (1972). *Education of the gifted and talented.* Washington, DC: Government Printing Office.

Middle States Association of Colleges and Secondary Schools. (1988). *Report of evaluating committee: Hunter College Campus Schools.* Unpublished manuscript.

Milgram, R.M. (1990). Creativity: An idea whose time has come and gone? In M.A. Runco & R.S. Albert (Eds.), *Theories of creativity* (pp. 215–233). Newbury Park, CA: Sage.

Milgram, R.M., & Milgram, N.A. (1976). Self-concept as a function of intelligence and creativity in gifted Israeli children. *Psychology in the Schools, 13,* 91–96.

National Association for Gifted Children. (1992). National Association for Gifted Children policy statement on ability grouping. *Gifted Child Quarterly, 36*(2).

Ochse, R. (1990). *Before the gates of excellence: The determinants of creative genius.* New York: Cambridge University Press.

Oden, M. (1968). A forty year follow-up of giftedness: Fulfillment and unfulfillment. *Genetic Psychology Monographs, 77,* 171–86.

Passow, A.H. (1985). Intellectual development of the gifted. In F.R. Link (Ed.), *Essays on the intellect* (pp. 23–43). Alexandria, VA: Association for Supervision and Curriculum Development.

Pletsch, C. (1991). *Young Nietzsche: Becoming a genius.* New York: Free Press.

Posner, M.I. (1988). What is it to be an expert? In M.T.H. Chi, R. Glaser, & M.J. Farr (Eds.), *The nature of expertise* (pp. xxix–xxvi). Hillsdale, NJ: Erlbaum.

Renzulli, J.S. (1986). The three-ring conception of giftedness: A developmental model for creative productivity. In R.J. Sternberg & J.E. Davidson (Eds.), *Conceptions of giftedness* (pp. 53–92). New York: Cambridge University Press.

Roe, A. (1953). *Making of a scientist.* New York: Dodd, Mead.

Sawyer, R.N. (1988). In defense of academic rigor. *Journal for the Education of the Gifted, 11*(2), 5–19.

Schopenhauer, A. (1966). *The world as will and representation* (Vol. 2, 2nd ed.). (Trans. by E.F.J. Payne). New York: Dover Books.

Schuster, D.T. (1986/7). *The interdependent mental stance: A study of gifted women at midlife* (Doctoral dissertation, The Claremont Graduate School, 1986). Dissertation Abstracts International, Vol. 48, 88A.

Schuster, D.T. (1990). Fulfillment of potential, life satisfaction, and competence: Comparing four cohorts of gifted women at midlife. *Journal of Educational Psychology, 82,* 471–478.

Scott, H.J. (1988). *Premises and principles that undergird educational policy at the Hunter College Campus Schools.* Unpublished manuscript.

Seagoe, M.V. (1975). *Terman and the gifted.* Los Altos, CA: W. Kaufmann.

Sears, P.S., & Barbee, A.H. (1975). Career and life satisfaction among Terman's gifted women. In J.C. Stanley, W.C. George, & C.H. Solano (Eds.), *The gifted and creative: A fifty–year perspective* (pp. 28–65). Baltimore, MD: Johns Hopkins University Press.

Sears, R.R. (1984). The Terman gifted children study. In S.A. Mednick, M. Hanway, & K.M. Finello (Eds.), *Handbook of longitudinal research. Volume 1: Birth and childhood cohorts* (pp. 398–414). New York: Praeger.

Sears, R.R. (1977). Sources of life satisfaction of the Terman gifted men. *American Psychologist, 32,* 119–128.

Shore, B.M., Cornell, D.G., Robinson, A., & Ward, V. (1991). *Recommended practices in gifted education: A critical analysis.* New York: Teachers College Press.

Simonton, D.K. (1990). History, chemistry, psychology and genius: An intellectual autobiography of historiometry. In M.A. Runco & R.S. Albert (Eds.), *Theories of creativity* (pp. 92–115). Newbury Park, CA: Sage.

Slavin, R.E. (1987). Grouping in the elementary school. *Educational Psychologist, 22,* 109–127.

Snyder, C.R., & Fromkin, H.L. (1980). *Uniqueness: The human pursuit of difference.* New York: Plenum Press.

Stanley, J., & Benbow, C. (1986). Youths who reason exceptionally well mathematically. In R. Sternberg & J. Davidson (Eds.), *Conceptions of giftedness* (pp. 361–387). New York: Cambridge University Press.

Sternberg, R.J. (1985). *Beyond IQ: A triarchic theory of human intelligence.* New York: Cambridge University Press.

Subotnik, R.F., & Arnold, K. (Eds.). (1993). *Beyond Terman: Longitudinal studies in contemporary gifted education.* Norwood, NJ: Ablex.

Subotnik, R.F., & Borland, J. (1992). Family factors in the adult success of high IQ children. *Illinois Council for the Gifted Journal, 11,* 37–42.

Subotnik, R.F., Karp, D.E., & Morgan, E.R. (1989). High-IQ children at midlife: An investigation into the generalizability of Terman's "Genetic Studies of Genius." *Roeper Review, 11*(3), 139–144.

Tannenbaum, A.J. (1983). *Gifted children: Psychological and educational perspectives.* New York: Macmillan.

Tannenbaum, A.J. (1986). Giftedness: A psychosocial approach. In R.J.

Sternberg & J.E. Davidson (Eds.), *Conceptions of giftedness* (pp. 21–52). New York: Cambridge University Press.

Terman, L.M. (1922). *Intelligence tests and school reorganization.* Yonkers-on-the-Hudson, NY: World Book.

Terman, L.M., & Oden, M.H. (1951). The Stanford studies of the gifted. In P.A. Witty (Ed.), *The gifted child* (pp. 20–46). Boston, MA: DC Heath.

Terman, L.M., & Oden, M.H. (1959). *The gifted group at midlife: Thirty-five years' follow-up of the superior child.* Stanford, CA: Stanford University Press.

Tomlinson-Keasey, C. (1990). Developing our intellectual resources for the 21st century: Educating the gifted. *Journal of Educational Psychology, 82*(3), 399–403.

Tomlinson-Keasey, C., & Little, T.D. (1990). Predicting educational attainment, occupational achievement, intellectual skill and personal adjustment among gifted men and women. *Journal of Educational Psychology, 82,* 442–455.

Van Tassel-Baska, J.L. (1988). *Comprehensive curriculum guide for gifted learners.* Boston, MA: Allyn & Bacon.

Van Tassel-Baska, J.L. (1989). Characteristics of the developmental path of eminent and gifted adults. In J.L. Van Tassel-Baska & P. Olszewski-Kubilius (Eds.), *Patterns of influence in gifted learners* (pp. 146–162). New York: Teachers College Press.

Waitzkin, F. (1988). *Searching for Bobby Fischer: The world of chess observed by the father of a child prodigy.* New York: Random House.

Walberg, H.J. (1988). Creativity and talent as learning. In R.J. Sternberg (Ed.), *The nature of creativity: Contemporary psychological perspectives* (pp. 340–361). New York: Cambridge University Press.

Walberg, H.J., Rasher, S.P., & Hase, K. (1983). IQ correlates with high eminence. In R.S. Albert (Ed.), *Genius and eminence: The social psychology of creativity and exceptional achievement* (pp. 52–56). Oxford: Pergamon Press.

White, W.L., & Renzulli, J.S. (1987). A forty-year follow-up of students who attended Leta Hollingworth's school for gifted students. *Roeper Review, 10*(2), 89–93.

Whitmore, J.R. (1980). *Giftedness, conflict and underachievement.* Boston, MA: Allyn & Bacon.

Witty, P. (1930). *One hundred gifted children.* Kansas City, KS: Kansas University Publications.

Zuckerman, H. (1983). The scientific elite: Nobel laureates' mutual influences. In R.S. Albert (Ed.), *Genius and eminence: The social psychology of creativity and exceptional achievement* (pp. 241–252). New York: Oxford University Press.

Author Index

Subject Index